A Workbook for Reading Argumentative Texts

A Workbook for Reading Argumentative Texts

Analytic Tools to Improve Understanding

James E. Scheuermann

ROWMAN & LITTLEFIELD
Lanham • Boulder • New York • London

Published by Rowman & Littlefield
An imprint of The Rowman & Littlefield Publishing Group, Inc.
4501 Forbes Boulevard, Suite 200, Lanham, Maryland 20706
www.rowman.com

86-90 Paul Street, London EC2A 4NE, United Kingdom

Copyright © 2022 by James E. Scheuermann

All rights reserved. No part of this book may be reproduced in any form or by any electronic or mechanical means, including information storage and retrieval systems, without written permission from the publisher, except by a reviewer who may quote passages in a review.

British Library Cataloguing in Publication Information Available

Library of Congress Cataloging-in-Publication Data

Names: Scheuermann, James, 1952- author.
Title: A workbook for reading argumentative texts : analytic tools to improve understanding / James E. Scheuermann.
Description: Lanham : Rowman & Littlefield, 2022. | Includes bibliographical references. | Summary: "This Workbook teaches the tools essential to analyzing and understanding the meaning of nonfiction texts that assert arguments"—Provided by publisher.
Identifiers: LCCN 2021050066 (print) | LCCN 2021050067 (ebook) | ISBN 9781475864731 (cloth) | ISBN 9781475864748 (paperback) | ISBN 9781475864755 (epub)
Subjects: LCSH: English language—Rhetoric—Problems, exercises, etc. | Reading comprehension—Problems, exercises, etc. | Persuasion (Rhetoric)—Problems, exercises, etc. | Critical thinking—Problems, exercises, etc. | LCGFT: Problems and exercises.
Classification: LCC PE1431 .S344 2021 (print) | LCC PE1431 (ebook) | DDC 160—dc23/eng/
20211128
LC record available at https://lccn.loc.gov/2021050066
LC ebook record available at https://lccn.loc.gov/2021050067

To my wife, Michalina, and our children, Beatrice and Peter
Without whom not

Contents

Preface	ix
Chapter 1: Introduction	1
Chapter 2: Reading Is Not a Spectator Sport	5
Chapter 3: Why Are You Reading?	7
Chapter 4: Arguments: A Closer Look	11
Chapter 5: Every Person Has a Skeleton, Every Argument Has a Structure	19
Chapter 6: What Does the Skeleton Look Like? Outlines and Summaries	25
Chapter 7: Ambiguity and Nonliteral Uses of Language	33
Chapter 8: Context Imparts Meaning	45
Chapter 9: The ABCs of Logic	59
Appendix A: Answer Key	69
Appendix B: Refugees Don't Undermine the US Economy—They Energize It *Ramya Vijaya*	111
Appendix C: The Disadvantages of an Elite Education *William Deresiewicz*	115

Appendix D: The Meaning of July 4 is Sacrifice 125
Carl J. Asszony

Appendix E: Antidotes for Fear 127
Martin Luther King Jr.

Appendix F: It's Time to End Any Level of Federal Marijuana
 Prohibition 137
Trevor Burrus

About the Author 141

Preface

This *Workbook* is a companion to *Reading Argumentative Texts: Analytic Tools to Improve Understanding* (which I will refer to as *Reading* in the remainder of this *Workbook*). Through exercises and case studies, this *Workbook* sharpens the analytical tools you have acquired through your study of *Reading*. In addition, certain of the exercises and case studies in this *Workbook* introduce new reading tools or invite you to deepen your analytical skills by applying the tools you now have to more difficult texts.

Two premises are at the heart of *Reading* and this *Workbook*. The first is that the meaning of an argumentative text is to be found not only in the statements that constitute the argument itself, but also in other statements that are irrelevant to the argument, that are only indirectly related to the argument, that give key terms in the argument additional meaning or obscure that meaning, or that make the argument more or less persuasive. The second premise is that there is no single, authoritative reading of an argumentative text.

The interplay of these two principles informs the view that analyzing and understanding an argumentative text is an art and that, within certain well-defined parameters, there are "better" and "worse" readings of a text and not "right" or "wrong" readings. Better readings are the product of better analytical skills. Better analytical skills lead to greater understanding. Greater understanding leads to a fuller, more meaningful, and more empowered life. This *Workbook* is intended to assist you on the path to that life.

The plan of this *Workbook* tracks that of *Reading*. In each chapter (with the exception of chapter 2, as you will see), the exercises and case studies refer back to and expand upon the lessons learned in the corresponding chapter of *Reading*. So, chapter 1 here refers to and applies the tools you acquired in chapter 1 of *Reading*, and similarly with each of the following chapters (with the exception of chapter 2). Each of the chapters here begins with a short summary of what you learned in the corresponding chapter of *Reading* followed by the exercises and, beginning in chapter 4, case studies.

The exercises vary in type and length. They include true-false questions, requests that you find in a text examples that illustrate a point made in *Reading*, requests that you create examples to illustrate a lesson taught in *Reading*, and opportunities to outline or summarize a text.

The case studies, like the exercises, sharpen and apply the tools you have acquired and, at times, expand your knowledge of how to use them. In addition, through my commentary and extended analyses, the case studies allow us to work together to wrestle the meaning out of a text or to determine that the text may not clearly express what the author meant. Think of the case studies as the questions we would be asking and the discussion we would be having if we were analyzing a text together in a classroom. Of course, in the classroom we would also be discussing practical advice to help you succeed in wrestling the meaning out of these texts, so that advice is included in our case studies here. Many of the case studies also propose lines of further inquiry if you are inclined to press your analysis of a text further than we do here.

As in *Reading*, the texts we employ here as the subjects of the exercises and case studies are drawn from a variety of sources, including opinion pieces from the mass media, historical documents, sermons, speeches, and selections from books. Some of the texts will be new to you and others very familiar. Your first reaction to encountering the familiar texts (like the *Gettysburg Address* and *Declaration of Independence*) may be that you know what these texts say and mean and that there is little to be gained from analyzing them in an exercise or case study. Please resist that reaction. I hope and expect that the analyses of these familiar texts with the tools you have acquired in *Reading* reveal new layers of meaning in them. When that occurs, you will have a greater appreciation of the richness of those texts and of the usefulness of the analytic tools you have mastered, and a new motivation to revisit other familiar texts to inquire what meanings may lie within that you previously missed.

The Answer Key at Appendix A of this *Workbook* contains answers, explanations, and discussions for most of the exercises and case studies. The explanations and discussions are intended to encourage you to consider and understand interpretations that may have not occurred to you and that may be "better" than those you developed. They also are intended to guide you, step-by-step, through some of the more difficult texts included here to reveal possible meanings and the nature, merits, and shortcomings of those texts from an argumentative perspective.

This *Workbook* is the product of the comments and criticisms of many readers and assistance from many other people. I have acknowledged these readers and other helpers in the Acknowledgements in *Reading*. I will not repeat their names here, but that does not lessen my deep gratitude for their many efforts to make this a better and more useful workbook than it otherwise would have been. The limits, imperfections, and errors in this *Workbook* are mine alone.

Read some good, heavy, serious books just for discipline: Take yourself in hand and master yourself.

—W.E.B. Du Bois (African American sociologist and civil rights leader, 1868–1963, in a letter written to his teenage daughter, 1914)

Chapter 1

Introduction

WHAT DO YOU KNOW?

You will recall that in chapter 1 of *Reading* you learned:
1. An argument is the form of reasoning that states a conclusion (or thesis) and attempts to show that it is true based on the truth of one or more other related statements, which are the premise or premises. In other words, any time an author asserts an argument in this sense, she is saying: "if these statements (the premises) are true, then this statement (the conclusion) is also true" or, "if you know that the premises are true (and I am telling you that they are), then you know that the conclusion is true."
2. The meaning of an argumentative text is the thoughts and emotions the author intends to communicate.
3. The principal sources of the meaning of an argumentative text are (a) the structure of the text, (b) the key sentences, words, and phrases in the text, (c) the context of the text, and (d) the logical relations between the statements in the text.
4. Virtually every writing that asserts an argument will have some statements that are part of the argument itself and other statements that are not part of the argument but which (a) give key terms in the argument additional meaning or obscure that meaning, (b) make parts of the argument more or less persuasive, (c) are only indirectly related to the argument, or (d) are not relevant to the argument at all. The meaning of an argumentative text is not found solely in the statements that constitute the argument, but also is found in the statements that are not part of the argument, and in the relations between the argumentative and non-argumentative statements.

5. There is a difference between a theoretical argument and a practical argument.

    a. A theoretical argument is an argument that is not intended to be action-guiding. It simply tries to prove that some fact, opinion, or belief is true ("Socrates is mortal").
    b. A practical argument is one that is intended to be action-guiding. It tells some person or entity what they or it should, ought, must, or needs to do. Practical arguments almost always contain or imply a premise that expresses a want, desire, need, or value ("you want to cool off"; "our government has a duty to stop climate change").

Let's try some exercises to flesh out what these lessons mean and to sharpen your understanding of them. After you have completed these exercises, compare your answers and analyses to the answers and discussion in the Answer Key in Appendix A.

EXERCISES

1.1. Are the following statements about arguments true or false?

   a. An "argument" is always verbal conflict, fighting with words, contradiction, or quarrel, especially an emotional one.
   b. The scribblings of a chimpanzee are a text.
   c. An argumentative text is a writing in which the author attempts to prove the truth of a conclusion based on the truth of one or more other statements, which are her premises.
   d. The conclusion of a practical argument is never an imperative (a command).
   e. No statement of objective fact can be the conclusion of a theoretical argument.
   f. For purposes of reading for understanding, "meaning" refers to the thoughts and emotions that the author intends to communicate to the reader.
   g. To understand the meaning of an argumentative text you need to understand the argument the text is stating.

1.2. Read the following paragraph. For ease of reference, I have numbered each sentence.
   [1] For years scientists puzzled over the cause of the extinction of the dinosaurs. [2] Our best scientific evidence tells us that around

Introduction 3

65 million years ago a massive asteroid hit the earth, sent millions of tons of ash, smoke, and debris into the atmosphere, blocked out most of the sun's rays, and caused the mass extinction of all of the dinosaurs and 90% of all other life forms. [3] The United States government is not prepared to prevent another gigantic asteroid from hitting the earth. [4] There is a substantial risk that such an impact could occur within the next 25 years. [5] If it does, it will end all civilization as we know it, cause billions of people to die painful, miserable, excruciating deaths, and, for any humans who are "lucky" enough to survive, existence will be like living in the Stone Age. [6] Our government needs to fund research on how to prevent another massive asteroid collision.

a. As we discussed in chapter 1 of *Reading*, not every nonfiction text or part of a nonfiction text states an argument. Does this paragraph assert an argument?

In order to answer that question, you need to determine whether any of the sentences state the author's premise or premises and whether any sentence states his conclusion. In other words, you need to ask yourself:

   i. is the author trying to prove something?
   ii. if so, what is it?
   iii. if so, what sentence (or sentences) states the point the author is trying to prove?
   iv. if he is trying to prove something, how does he do so?
   v. what sentences state his reasons for the conclusion of his argument?

If you are struggling to answer these questions, maybe that is because the author does not make an argument in this passage. Or, maybe it is because this is a tough paragraph to analyze and you need more practice. In either case, do not get discouraged. You are just getting started at this and we will work through the tough spots together.

b. If you think the author is making an argument, restate the argument as we did in chapter 1 of *Reading*, with premises and a conclusion, like this:

_____[Premise]
_____[Premise]
_____[And so on, if necessary.]
_____[Conclusion]

c. Are there any sentences in this paragraph that are not part of your argument? If so, why did the author include them in this text?
d. If you think the author is making an argument, is it a theoretical or practical argument?
e. If you think the author is not making an argument, write down the reasons why you think there is no argument in this passage.
f. If we were to drill down a bit more, there is a host of questions you could ask yourself about this passage. Take a look at sentence [5]. It talks about the "painful, miserable, excruciating deaths" of billions of people. Assuming that the passage is making an argument, are the adjectives "painful, miserable, excruciating" necessary to the argument? In other words, could the author still draw the same conclusion even without them? Are they simply rhetorical, that is, are they included solely to produce an emotional reaction in the reader? What do they add, if anything, to proving the conclusion that the fact of billions of people dying does not already contribute?
g. Again, assume the passage is making an argument. Is this clause in sentence [6]—"for any humans who survive, existence will be like living in the Stone Age"—a necessary part of the reasoning from the other premises to the conclusion? If it is not necessary, is it included in an argumentative paragraph for rhetorical impact? Is it included only to illustrate what the "end of all civilization" means? Does it cause visions of Neanderthals, cave dwellers, and post-apocalyptic movies to come to mind, whereas "the end of civilization" does not quite do that so forcefully or clearly?

1.3. Give an example of a theoretical argument, other than one you read in *Reading*. This could be an example you make up yourself or one that you read somewhere other than in the text of Reading.
1.4. Give an example of a practical argument, other than one you read in Reading. Again, this could be an example you make up yourself or one that you read somewhere other than in the text of *Reading*.

Chapter 2

Reading Is Not a Spectator Sport

EXERCISES

Most of the exercises in this *Workbook* allow you to apply and test the tools you have learned in the corresponding chapters of *Reading*. Here, the exercises are slightly different. The exercises below anticipate one of the lessons taught in chapter 6 of *Reading*. Doing these few exercises now will give you a baseline against which to measure your progress in becoming a better reader.

We will start by thinking about what a summary is and why it is useful.

2.1. Defining terms is usually a good way to clarify your thinking. So:

  a. In your own words, define the term "summary."
  b. Compare your definition to one or more dictionary definitions.
  c. Is your definition incomplete when compared to the dictionary definition?
  d. Does the dictionary offer a definition that seems to apply most appropriately to summarizing an argumentative text? Make a note of that definition.

In the Answer Key at the end of this *Workbook*, you will find a quick and ready definition of "summary" that you can use for purposes of the exercises in this chapter. We refine that definition in chapter 6 of *Reading*.

2.2. Ask yourself, what is chapter 2 of *Reading* trying to accomplish? What is the point of the chapter? How does chapter 2 attempt to accomplish that goal?

2.3. With those answers and your definition of "summary" in mind:

    a. Summarize the main point of the first section of chapter 2.
    b. Summarize the main point of the second section of chapter 2.
    c. Summarize the main point of the third section of chapter 2.

If you have never summarized a text before, that is not a problem. You can realistically expect your first efforts at this to be a bit rough. Give it a try anyhow.

2.4. After reading chapter 6 of *Reading*, come back here, review your summaries and ask yourself:

    a. what have I learned about summarizing a text that I did not know when I did the summaries of chapter 2?
    b. how could my summaries of the sections of chapter 2 be improved?

2.5. If you find yourself taking shortcuts in your college reading, is it because you are afraid you cannot get all of the reading done on time? If so, you are not unique. It is a common problem. Know this: fear generally is a poor motive for learning something, and generally a poor teacher.

    Whatever your motivation in reading *Reading* or this *Workbook*, if you find yourself pressed for time, schedule a block (or blocks) of time every day for reading and stick to it. Getting control of your reading schedule will allow you to give each assigned reading the attention it deserves. Time is a finite resource. You cannot create more of it. All you can do is get control over it. When you do that, your reading will be more productive and more enjoyable.

    Find a friend and compare your schedule with his or hers. See any room for improvement in yours?

Chapter 3

Why Are You Reading?

WHAT DO YOU KNOW?

In chapter 3 of *Reading* we discussed three principal purposes of reading: (a) reading for understanding; (b) reading for information; and (c) reading to become wise. Specifically, you learned:

1. Within a zone of reasonableness, there is no test or rule by which it can be determined for all purposes that a reading of an argumentative text is authoritatively (beyond dispute) "right" or "wrong." There is no one authoritative reading of a text. There are only readings that are better (more careful, more nuanced, and more insightful) and worse (less careful, less nuanced, and less insightful).
2. A reading is outside of the zone of reasonableness if the reading:

    a. Is contradicted by or is contrary to what the author expressly states.
    b. Cannot be inferred from (is not implied by) what the author expressly states.
    c. Is not directly contradictory to what the author expressly states, but is grossly incomplete. It does not acknowledge much of what the author has actually written.
    d. Commits the author to a nonsensical or obviously factually false position.

3. There is always a place for criticism of an author's opinions or the way he presents, or fails to present, evidence to support his views. The proper role of criticism is to be an aid to understanding or a result of

understanding. It is not a goal to be achieved by skipping understanding altogether.
4. Reading a text for particular bits of information and knowing how to obtain information from a text is different from understanding an argument and the meaning of the text in which it is embedded.
5. Reading to be wise is not the same as reading to understand the meaning of an argumentative text. There are no tools that allow you to extract wisdom from a text, but there are tools that allow you to wrestle meaning from a text and to understand it better.

The exercises in this chapter are designed to reinforce the differences between these three purposes and to test what you have learned about reading for understanding.

EXERCISES

3.1. True or false:

   a. There is always one correct restatement of "the argument" of a text that a reader can point to and say with no doubt, "this is the argument and nothing else in the text is part of the argument."
   b. Argumentative texts are subject to multiple interpretations (different readings).
   c. The "zone of reasonableness" test allows a reader to determine which reading of an argumentative text is authoritatively (beyond dispute) "right" or "wrong."
   d. There are only three purposes in reading, namely, reading for understanding, reading to obtain information, and reading to gain wisdom.

3.2. You learned that a reading that cannot be inferred from (is not implied by) what the author expressly states is outside of the zone that makes an interpretation of an argumentative text reasonable. State in your own words what this means.

3.3. What is the purpose of reading for understanding?

3.4. Consider this passage from the British novelist and essayist Virginia Woolf:

> Do not dictate to your author; try to become him. Be his fellow-worker and accomplice. If you hang back, . . . and criticize at first, you are preventing yourself from getting the fullest possible value from what you read. But if you open your mind as widely as possible, then signs and hints of almost imperceptible fineness, from the

twist and turn of the first sentences, will bring you into the presence of a human being unlike any other.[1]

Is this a reasonably accurate description of what it means to read for understanding, to read for information, to read to become wise, or none of these? Explain your answer.

3.5. As you work through the exercises in the rest of this book, ask yourself whether your reading of each text satisfies the criteria that define the zone of reasonableness.

NOTE

1. Virginia Woolf, "How Should One Read a Book?" in *The Virginia Woolf Reader*, p. 235 (New York: Harcourt, Inc. 1984, Mitchell A. Leaska, ed.).

Chapter 4

Arguments
A Closer Look

WHAT DO YOU KNOW?

In chapter 4 of *Reading* we took a deeper dive into the nature of arguments. Among the things you learned there were:

1. Why two myths about arguments are incorrect.

    Myth #1: The conclusion of an argument must be a statement of a subjective opinion.
    In truth, the conclusion of an argument can be a statement of subjective opinion or a statement of objective fact.
    Myth #2. The conclusion of an argument must be a statement that can be proven true or false because it asserts that some state of affairs ("the earth is round") is or is not real.
    In truth, the conclusion of one type of argument, a practical argument, is a direction or command to do something ("drive slowly") or a statement as to how some person or entity should act ("you ought to drive more slowly," "our government should stop spying on us").

2. The distinction between deductive and inductive arguments.

    a. A deductive argument is one in which the conclusion is said to follow necessarily from its premises, whatever else may be true in the world.

b. An *inductive argument* is one in which the conclusion is said to follow from the premises only probably, and with the implication that other facts in the world could require that the conclusion be modified or abandoned. Inductive arguments usually are grounded in data, evidence, or facts, and more or different data, evidence, or facts could change the conclusion.

3. A *valid deductive argument* is one in which the conclusion does necessarily follow from its premises; there is no way for the premises to be true and the conclusion to be false. An *invalid deductive argument* is one in which the conclusion does not necessarily follow from its premises; the premises may be true and yet the conclusion may be false.
4. A *strong inductive argument* is one in which the conclusion follows from the premises with a high probability or likelihood; it is more likely than not that if the premises are true the conclusion is true. A *weak inductive argument* is one in which the conclusion follows from the premises with a low probability or likelihood; the premises often refer to a small set of evidence or attempt to reason from a weak analogy between two or more things.
5. An *enthymeme* or *enthymatic argument* is one in which one or more of the premises is unstated and only implied.
6. There are four types of arguments: (a) deductive-practical, (b) deductive-theoretical, (c) inductive-practical, and (d) inductive-theoretical.
7. In addition to argumentative nonfiction texts, there are four other types of nonfiction writing, namely, expository, descriptive, explanatory, and rhetorical.

EXERCISES

4.1. True or false:

   a. All deductive arguments have general premises and a particular conclusion.
   b. All inductive arguments contain particular premises and a general conclusion.
   c. Some deductive arguments are weak.
   d. Some inductive arguments are weak.
   e. All inductive arguments are valid.
   f. Some inductive arguments are strong and some are invalid.
   g. All valid deductive arguments contain only true premises.

h. All invalid deductive arguments contain only false premises.
i. A valid deductive argument can contain false premises and a false conclusion.
j. The conclusion of an inductive argument must be a statement of subjective opinion.
k. The conclusion of a deductive argument can be a statement of subjective opinion.
l. A deductive argument that commits an error in reasoning is called an invalid argument.
m. An inductive argument that does not commit an error in reasoning is called a valid argument.
n. A text that offers an explanation of an event can assert an argument.
o. Every enthymatic argument is invalid.
p. Every enthymatic argument is strong.
q. Inductive arguments always reason from particular premises to general conclusions.
r. Deductive arguments always reason from general premises to particular conclusions.
s. The conclusion of a valid deductive argument can be false.
t. The premises of a valid deductive argument can be false.
u. Any argument in which the conclusion is stated first and the premises follow it is invalid.
v. Some inductive arguments reason from particular premises to general conclusions.
w. Some deductive arguments reason from general premises to particular conclusions.

4.2. Develop an example that shows that Myth #1 is incorrect, other than one found in *Reading*. This is a tough exercise.

To work through it, think about how you use deductive or inductive reasoning every day. For example, suppose you are in a grocery store and are looking for ketchup. You are thinking, what aisle has the ketchup? You would formulate an argument to answer this question with an objective fact (the ketchup is in aisle 4, or, the ketchup probably is in aisle 4). The premises that would lead you to that objective conclusion would be something like these:

The mustard and relish are in aisle 4.
Mustard and relish are condiments.
Ketchup is a condiment.
All of the condiments are usually kept in the same aisle of the grocery store.
And your conclusion (of this inductive argument) would be:

So, the ketchup probably is in aisle 4.

4.3. Develop an example that shows that Myth #2 is incorrect, other than one found in *Reading*.

4.4. Restate each of the following enthymatic arguments formally, *i.e.*, with the premise(s) first and then the conclusion, and fill in the missing premise:

   a. Of course he's good at basketball. He practices every day.
   b. I don't trust Donald. Every time we talk, he lies to me.
   c. Eric is a liar and a crook. Anyone who belongs to that family is a liar and a crook.
   d. All good Communists have studied the works of Karl Marx. So, you are not a good Communist.

4.5. Create an example of an enthymatic argument, other than one found in *Reading*.

4.6. Suppose you read a text that looked like it was making an argument, but it did not expressly state a conclusion based on the sentences in the text which you understood to be premises. However, a conclusion could be implied from those premises. Would that text be making an enthymatic argument? Why or why not?

4.7. The wonderful Kentucky writer Wendell Berry begins one of his essays with this paragraph:

> I live in Henry County, near the lower end of the Kentucky River Valley, on a small farm that is half woodland. Starting from my backdoor, I could walk for days and never leave the woods except to cross the roads. Though Henry County is known as farming country, 25 percent of it is wooded. From the hillside behind my house I can see thousands of acres of trees in the counties of Henry, Owen, and Carroll.[1]

   a. Does this paragraph, state an argument? Is Berry trying to reason from premises to a conclusion?
   b. If so, restate the argument he is making by identifying the premises and conclusion.
   c. If not, what kind of nonfiction writing is this?

4.8. Read the essay, "Some Convenient Truths," by Gregg Easterbrook (available at, Some Convenient Truths–The Atlantic). What kind of nonfiction writing is this—argumentative, descriptive, explanatory, expository?

   Before attempting to answer this question, it is helpful to be very clear about the subject of this essay. Is the subject: (a) possible solutions to global warming, (b) historical attempts to solve the problem of air pollution, or (c) something else?

4.9. Read the op-ed essay, "Who gets care for COVID-19 when hospitals fill up? Gut-wrenching decisions will have to be made" (available at http://www.chicagotribune.com/opinion/commentary/ct-opinion-coronavirus-hospital-care-decisions-20200330-ci5h3kebfrdj7jlesnbqbgzpdq-story.html). By way of context, the essay was first published on March 30, 2020, early in the spread of the COVID-19 pandemic in the United States and before infections and deaths had peaked in any state.

   a. Examine this text carefully. It is an argumentative essay. Does it contain one or more arguments? To answer this question, it would be best to start by asking how many conclusions does the essay argue for? Once you have answered that question, you know how many arguments the essay articulates. Alternatively, to answer this question, restate the argument(s) the essay makes. Because of the style in which the essay is written, you will not find it easy to restate its argument (or arguments).
   b. Are the argument(s) inductive, deductive, or both?

4.10. Read the essay, "Refugees don't undermine the US economy—they energize it," attached at Appendix B.[2]

   a. State the thesis of the argument of this essay. What premises lead to that conclusion?
   b. Is this a deductive or an inductive argument? Why?
   c. If it is inductive, is it strong or weak? If it is deductive, is it valid or invalid? Why?

4.11. Recall this passage from chapter 2 of *Reading:*

   You may think about reading along these lines: (1) football players play the game and I am a spectator passively watching them play, (2) similarly, the author has written the book and I passively soak up (read) what she has written, (3) watching football requires not being distracted (especially if it is an important game), (4) reading requires not being distracted, so (5) reading is like watching football.

   a. State the thesis of the argument of this paragraph.
   b. Is this a deductive or inductive argument? Why?
   c. Is it valid, invalid, strong, or weak? Why?

CASE STUDY: THE *GETTYSBURG ADDRESS*

Lincoln's *Gettysburg Address* is one of the most important documents in American history. Yet it is remarkably short. Here is the complete text.[3]

> Four score and seven years ago our fathers brought forth on this continent a new nation, conceived in Liberty, and dedicated to the proposition that all men are created equal.
>
> Now we are engaged in a great civil war, testing whether that nation, or any nation so conceived and so dedicated, can long endure. We are met on a great battle-field of that war. We have come to dedicate a portion of that field as a final resting place for those who here gave their lives that that nation might live. It is altogether fitting and proper that we should do this.
>
> But, in a larger sense, we can not dedicate—we can not consecrate—we can not hallow—this ground. The brave men, living and dead, who struggled here, have consecrated it, far above our poor power to add or detract. The world will little note, nor long remember what we say here, but it can never forget what they did here. It is for us the living, rather, to be dedicated here to the unfinished work which they who fought here have thus far so nobly advanced. It is rather for us to be here dedicated to the great task remaining before us—that from these honored dead we take increased devotion to that cause for which they gave the last full measure of devotion—that we here highly resolve that these dead shall not have died in vain—that this nation, under God, shall have a new birth of freedom—and that government of the people, by the people, for the people, shall not perish from the earth.

4.12. Analyze this text using the tools you learned in chapter 4 of *Reading*.

  a. Is this an argumentative text? If so, restate the argument(s) it makes.
  b. If you read the *Address* as stating an argument, what kind of argument does it make?
  c. There are clearly rhetorical phrases, sentences, and passages in this speech. Identify at least three of them.
  d. Apart from its rhetorical aspects, does the speech have one or more elements of the other three types of nonargumentative nonfiction writing (exposition, description, explanation) that we discussed in chapter 4 of *Reading*? If so, identify the passages that contain these elements.

NOTES

1. Wendell Berry, "Conserving Forest Communities," in *Wendell Berry Essays 1993–2017* (New York: Library of America, 2019, Jack Shoemaker ed.).

2. Also available at Refugees don't undermine the US economy – they energize it (theconversation.com).

3. You can find this speech in many history books and in many online sites, *e.g.*, http://www.abrahamlincolnonline.org/lincoln/speeches/gettysburg.htm.

Chapter 5

Every Person Has a Skeleton, Every Argument Has a Structure

WHAT DO YOU KNOW?

In chapter 5 of *Reading*, you learned the purpose of an introduction, six different kinds of introductions, and how an introduction may or may not give you clear guidance about the meaning of the author's argument. Specifically, you learned:

1. Virtually every argumentative text—whether it is an article, essay, book, historical account, or something else—has an introduction, a middle, and a conclusion. (There may be rare exceptions to this proposition.) As the term "introduction" suggests, the introduction usually comes at or near the beginning of the work.
2. In the most rigorous argumentative pieces, the introduction typically (a) includes a statement of the author's thesis and (b) tells the reader the plan of the work, how generally she is going to prove her thesis, including the major points the author is going to make to prove it. The introduction in effect says, "here's the destination (my thesis) and here's the map to show you how I'm going to get there (the plan or structure of my argument)." This is the Road Map introduction.
3. The other types of introductions we discussed were:

    a. The "Subject Variation" on the Road Map

        i. The author introduces his work by stating the subject matter he is going to discuss, but not his thesis or plan of argument regarding that subject matter.

b. Asking a Question (Stating a Problem)

   i. The author introduces his work by asking a question or, equivalently, stating a problem.

c. The Anecdotal Introduction

   i. The author introduces her work by recounting an anecdote (a short story) to lead her readers into a discussion of a larger point.

d. Let's Get Right to the Point

   i. The author introduces her work by immediately stating her thesis and then arguing for it.

e. Just the Facts, Ma'am, Just the Facts

   i. The author introduces his work by reciting some body of facts or data thought to be relevant to his thesis and argument.

4. The six types of introductions identified above are not exhaustive of the types of introductions you may encounter. They are some of the most common. If you cannot find one of these introductions, or some other form of introduction in a text, it should raise the question in your mind whether you are reading argumentative text or some other form of nonfiction writing.

EXERCISES

5.1. Go back to the *Gettysburg Address,* which we analyzed in chapter 4 above. What kind of introduction does the text employ?

5.2. The many issues relating to war and peace are not going to go away in your lifetime. Recognizing this, scholars continue to write serious treatises on how to prevent wars and on the conditions needed for peace. Consider this introduction to one such book.

> This book is about the modern state—how it came into being, how it has developed, and in what directions we can expect it to change. Wars, especially those . . . conflicts that often extend over decades, have been critical to the birth and development of the state, and

> therefore much of this book is concerned with the history of warfare. Equally determinative of the state has been its legal order, and so this book is about law.¹

This is not the easiest paragraph to read or to understand. Nonetheless, you can answer this question: what type of introduction does this paragraph employ? What words in this paragraph are you relying on to support your answer?

5.3. The great British philosopher Bertrand Russell wrote a short introduction to philosophy entitled, *The Problems of Philosophy*. He begins the final chapter of that book with this paragraph.

> Having now come to the end of our brief . . . review of the problems of philosophy, it will be well to consider . . . what is the value of philosophy and why it ought to be studied. It is the more necessary to consider this question, in view of the fact that many men, under the influence of science or practical affairs, are inclined to doubt whether philosophy is anything better than innocent but useless trifling, hair-splitting distinctions, and controversies on matters concerning which knowledge is impossible.²

What kind of introduction is this?

5.4. Read this introduction to a book on violence:

> In this book, I will demonstrate that the most obvious form of violence—seen in acts of crime and terror, civil unrest, international conflict, and the like—is only one of three kinds of violence. In addition to this "subjective" form of violence, there is "symbolic" violence embodied in our language and other meaning systems. Finally, there is also "systemic" violence, which is the violence embedded in our economic and political systems.
>
> I will demonstrate this by showing, first, that many of those who combat subjective violence commit systemic violence that generates subjective violence; second that violence is caused by fear of others, which itself is founded in our language; [and so on with other points we will omit, since they are not relevant here].
>
> This analysis teaches us three lessons. First, to chastise violence is to make an ideological statement that reinforces the invisibility of symbolic and systemic violence. Second, it is difficult to be violent in a way that disturbs the fundamental aspects of social life. Finally, violence is not a property of acts, but of acts and their contexts.³

What kind of introduction is this? State why.

5.5. Read the essay "The Disadvantages of an Elite Education." An edited version is attached at Appendix C.⁴ What type of introduction does this essay contain?

5.6. Re-read the introduction to chapter 1 of *Reading*. What kind of introduction is it?

5.7. Read Dr. Martin Luther King's essay, "Letter from a Birmingham Jail."[5] This essay, styled as a "letter," is a classic defense of illegal, nonviolent protest and also is a classic of the 20th century civil rights movement in the United States. It is a response to a public statement signed by eight white clergymen regarding the nonviolent protests that Dr. King was leading in Birmingham, Alabama in 1963. The essay is somewhat unusual in that it is a rebuttal to arguments made in the statement of the clergymen, but that statement is almost never published alongside of Dr. King's letter. Accordingly, the reader of Dr. King's Letter is compelled to reconstruct what the clergymen's statement said. That is not difficult given the clarity of Dr. King's response, but it does require an extra step on your part.

   a. Identify the introduction to the Letter. Is the introduction an example of one of the six types of introductions we discussed in chapter 5 of *Reading*?
   b. Restate the introduction in your own words.
   c. Does Dr. King state a thesis anywhere in this text?
   d. Is he trying to prove one or many points? That is, does he have one thesis or more than one?
   e. Assume he has just one major point he is trying to prove, one thesis. State in your own words the one major point this Letter is trying to prove.

5.8. Re-read the essay, "Refugees don't undermine the US economy—they energize it," attached at Appendix B.[6] What kind of introduction does this essay employ?

5.9. Suppose the following paragraph is the introduction to a 4th of July newspaper editorial:

> We all love fireworks, beer, hot dogs, and parades on the 4th of July. It is a true American holiday, our national birthday. In the midst of these mid-summer rituals, we should not forget that the 4th of July is most importantly a celebration of patriotism. The standard Merriam-Webster *Dictionary* defines "patriotism" as "love for or devotion to one's country." Many Americans give meaning to this word every day through their actions. On this 4th of July, let's look at how a few of these Americans define "patriotism" through their conduct at home, on the job, and in their volunteer activities.

Is this introduction an example of one of the six kinds of introduction we studied in chapter 5 of *Reading*? If so, what kind is it? If not, how would you describe this kind of introduction?

Every Person Has a Skeleton, Every Argument Has a Structure 23

CASE STUDY: AN OP-ED ON THE MEANING OF THE 4TH OF JULY

Many newspapers acknowledge our principal secular and religious holidays through editorials or op-ed pieces. Newspaper readers typically encounter such reflections on the significance of a holiday in editorial pages on New Year's Day, Memorial Day, the 4th of July, Thanksgiving, and Christmas. In this case study, we examine one such text, an op-ed piece from a New Jersey newspaper reflecting on July 4th. Specifically, the initial focus of this case study is to ask what an introduction may tell us about whether a text is argumentative or is one of the other types of nonfiction writing we discussed in chapter 4.

    5.10. Read "True meaning of July 4 is sacrifice," attached at Appendix D.[7]

        It is instructive to ask, first, whether this text has one of the six types of introductions we discussed in chapter 5 of *Reading*. Let's assume that it may be best read as having a "let's get right to the point" type of introduction. The first sentence appears to state an opinion that is intended to support the second sentence, which apparently states a thesis. That would seem to be fairly simple and straightforward. But does that reading of the first paragraph square with the rest of the text?

       a. If the last sentence of the first paragraph states the thesis of the text, then we would expect to find in the rest of the piece propositions in support of that thesis. Identify the statements in the text that the author uses (or may use) to support the statement that the "real meaning" of the 4th of July is "gradually being forgotten."
       b. The title of the op-ed states that the "True meaning of July 4 is sacrifice." Identify the statements that the author uses to support this statement.
       c. Assume that there is one "true meaning" of July 4th, as the author believes. Does the evidence relied upon by this author demonstrate that he has identified that one "true meaning"? Could this author or another author rely on other historical or current events to argue for a different "true meaning" of July 4th?

        For example, how many other countries were born and survived because of the self-sacrifice of their leading citizens or of the great mass of their citizens? If the United States is not unique in this regard, then why is sacrifice the meaning of July 4th and not also the meaning of the date of the founding of every nation?

        Are there other candidates for the "true meaning" of July 4th? Consider whether the "true meaning" of July 4th may be that for the first time in history a nation dedicated itself (at least in writing) to "unalienable rights," to life, liberty, the pursuit of happiness, and equality for all. Or, consider whether the "true meaning" of July 4th in 21st century America is that after more than 200 years, human rights, liberty, and equality are ideals that we only imperfectly realize in our institutions.

    d. Assume that this is an argumentative text. What is the thesis of this essay? Is it found in the title, in the last sentence of the first paragraph, in both places, or somewhere else?

5.11. When you have answered these questions, step back and ask: what do my answers tell me about whether this text is attempting to assert an argument (or two), or whether the piece is intended to be one of the other forms of nonfiction texts we examined at the end of chapter 4 of *Reading*?

NOTES

1. Philip Bobbitt, *The Shield of Achilles*, p. xxi (New York: Anchor Books 2003). I have revised and edited this paragraph slightly.

2. Bertrand Russell, *The Problems of Philosophy*, p. 153 (London: Oxford U. Press 1969).

3. Slavoj Zizek, *Violence*, pp. 1–8, 206–17 (New York: Picador 2008). You will not find these paragraphs in the early pages of *Violence*. I have reconstructed them from several passages in the book to provide a clear example of one type of introduction you may encounter in a work on politics or sociology.

4. The complete essay is available at, https://theamericanscholar.org/the-disadvantages-of-an-elite-education/#.XkQa7Y3saQU.

5. Available at, https://www.africa.upenn.edu/Articles_Gen/Letter_Birmingham.html. You can find the document at many sites on the internet, but be aware that there are substantive and stylistic differences among the various texts.

6. Also available at, Refugees don't undermine the US economy – they energize it (theconversation.com).

7. Also available at, https://www.dailyrecord.com/story/opinion/editorials/2018/07/03/editorial-true-meaning-july-sacrifice/36592701/.

Chapter 6

What Does the Skeleton Look Like?
Outlines and Summaries

WHAT DO YOU KNOW?

In chapter 6 of *Reading* you learned:

1. The purpose of an outline is to show the structure of a text. Typically, it sets forth, *in the same order in which the text presents them*:

    a. the principal points the text is making; some of these points will be part of the author's argument and some may not be,
    b. the evidence (*i.e.,* the facts, scientific studies, anecdotes, opinions of others, analysis of concepts, etc.) that the author uses to support the main points of his argument, and
    c. the relationships between the points the author is making and the evidence presented to support those points (through the use of sub-points and sub-sub-points).

2. Argumentative texts in the mass media almost never proceed in a strictly logical progression. The premises and conclusion (thesis) of an argument often are scattered about the text.
3. In analyzing an argumentative text for its meaning you will need to determine what the argument is, what else is included in the text that is not part of the argument, why those other parts are included, and what those other parts do to the argument, if anything (make it more or less clear, give some parts additional emphasis, add emotional appeals, and so on). One of the best ways to do that is to do an outline of the piece.

4. A summary of an argumentative text communicates your understanding of the main elements of a text. For a reader who is trying to understand an argumentative text, a summary is a useful way of stepping back and asking: what is the point of the text? what do I know about the text?
5. As a general matter, your summary of longer works should state:

   a. the name of the author,
   b. the title of the work you are summarizing,
   c. the author's thesis,
   d. the main points he made in attempting to prove the thesis, and
   e. a mention of the evidence or *types* of evidence he employs.

   There are exceptions to these five points, as you will recall.

The following exercises invite you to use these tools to analyze the meaning of several texts we have encountered so far and a few new texts as well.

EXERCISES

6.1. Summarize the article on studying Latin, discussed in chapter 6 of *Reading*.

6.2. Go back to the exercises for chapter 2 above.

   a. Review the summaries you wrote in answering the exercises for chapter 2 above.
   b. How could these summaries be improved in light of what you have learned in chapter 6 of *Reading*? Rewrite them now in light of what you have learned about outlines and summaries.

6.3. Read the opinion piece, "The end of a U.S.-Russia arms treaty spells long-term trouble."[1]

   a. Outline this essay.
   b. Identify the thesis and premises for the thesis.
   c. Summarize this article.

6.4. Go back to Dr. King's essay, "Letter from a Birmingham Jail,"[2] which we encountered in the exercises for chapter 5 above.

a. Outline the essay.

You likely will find this essay harder to outline than some of the others we have been analyzing. You may interpret this essay to be no more than a rambling walk through many different topics, with little or no connection between them. If that is your reaction on the first or second reading of the text, that may be because reading the essay is like hearing only one side of an ongoing dialogue, since you do not have the statement of the clergymen that Dr. King is responding to.

What do you do in those circumstances? Give special attention to each of the points Dr. King is rebutting or responding to. For example, the second, third, and fourth paragraphs are all directed to the clergymen's apparent argument (or statement) that Dr. King and his fellow protesters are "outsiders coming in" to stir up trouble or violence in Birmingham. The fifth paragraph responds to a separate point made by the clergymen, apparently one deploring the very fact that the demonstrations were occurring at all. And so on.

Once you have outlined each of the major points that Dr. King makes in responding to points made by the clergymen, then you can organize each of the remaining paragraphs as stating subpoints supporting Dr. King's rebuttals.

b. Summarize the essay.

6.5. Re-read the essay "The Disadvantages of an Elite Education." An edited version is attached at Appendix C.[3]

    a. Outline the essay.
    b. Summarize the essay.
    c. Is this an argumentative text or one of the other forms of nonfiction writing we discussed in chapter 4 of *Reading*?
    d. If it is an argumentative text, what kind of argument does it make: (i) deductive-theoretical, (ii) deductive-practical, (iii) inductive-theoretical, or (iv) inductive-practical?

6.6. Re-read our discussion in chapter 6 of *Reading* of Ms. Deutsch's essay on lowering the voting age ("Ayanna Pressley Is Right: 16-Year-Olds Deserve the Right to Vote," attached at Appendix B of *Reading*[4]). Focus in particular on our discussion of paragraph 5 in our outline of the text (which analyzes paragraphs 8 through 14 of the article).

    a. What parts of her argument in paragraphs 8 through 14 of the article would you rearrange or omit to make the argument stronger, if any?

What type of evidence would you attempt to uncover through research and add to the article to strengthen the argument?

CASE STUDY: DR. KING'S "ANTIDOTES FOR FEAR"

You will recall that in chapter 5 of *Reading* we touched briefly on Dr. King's introduction to his sermon, "Antidotes for fear." This text is especially instructive because its structure is clear and explicit, which is not common in works for the general public. Accordingly, it is a good example of how the structure of a text communicates meaning and how an outline assists the reader in understanding both the argument that a text is making and the other parts of the text that may or may not add meaning to that argument.

Read the sermon, which is reprinted in Appendix E.

6.7. It will be helpful for you to start by summarizing the sermon. If you are finding this challenging, that is to be expected. Try it, and we will revisit your summary later to see how it may be improved after you have done an outline.

6.8. As we noted in chapter 5 of *Reading*, Dr. King's introduction to the sermon is long relative to the length of the entire sermon. Dr. King must have had a reason for this.

   a. What does this introduction tell you about the substance of the sermon? Does it present the thesis and plan of an argument, introduce an argument, make an argument, or do something else?
   b. Where would you start to try to answer these questions? You know that outlining is a great tool, so let's start there. A detailed outline of the introduction looks like this:

   1. Every person experiences the depression and bewilderment of crippling fear. [Paragraph 1]
   2. Men and women everywhere fear poor physical and mental health. [Paragraph 2]
   3. Fear spawns phobias, *i.e.*, more fears. [Paragraph 3]
   4. Our competitive economic system creates fears of unemployment and business failures. [Paragraph 4]
   5. We fear nuclear annihilation. [Paragraph 5]
   6. We should not seek to eliminate fear altogether, even if it were possible. [Paragraph 7]

      a. As an elemental alarm system of human beings, fear has survival benefits and is a normal, necessary, and creative force.

i. It has caused us to discover electricity, to make advances in medicine, to build institutions of learning, and to found institutions of peace like the United Nations.

7. Abnormal fears are emotionally and psychologically destructive and paralyze us. [Paragraphs 8 and 9]
8. Normal fear protects us and motivates us to improve our individual and collective welfare. [Paragraph 9]
9. Because fear cannot be eliminated and normal fear is beneficial, our task is to master it. [Paragraph 9]
10. The rest of this sermon will show you how it can be mastered. (The rest of the sermon will answer the question, "How may it be mastered?") [Paragraph 9]

Because Dr. King writes clearly and his argument is relatively easy to follow, this outline is fairly straightforward and generally follows the point or points of each paragraph in the introduction. What is of special interest now is that by doing this outline of the introduction, you see that Dr. King's sermon has two major parts, each of which contains a separate argument. The first major part is the introduction itself, where Dr. King argues that fear cannot be eliminated, that we should not want to eliminate some fears because they are beneficial, and so we can only master our fears. The second major part of the sermon is everything in the next four sections, where he argues that there are four techniques for mastering fear.

Let's consider this point in further detail. The argument of the introduction can be stated, in this simplified form:

Everyone everywhere lives in some form of fear. [Premise]
    Men and women fear poor physical and mental health, unemployment and business failures, and nuclear annihilation. [Sub-premise]
Some fears are harmful and some are beneficial. [Premise]
    Fear is an elemental alarm system of human beings, has survival benefits, and is a normal, necessary, and creative force. [Sub-premise]
    Abnormal fears are emotionally and psychologically destructive and paralyze us. [Sub-premise]
In either case, no one can eliminate fear altogether from his or her life. [Premise]
Accordingly, we can only learn to master fear. [Conclusion]

The sub-premises articulate the supporting evidence for each premise. This argument could be fleshed out with additional sub-premises, but we need not go into that level of detail here.

Having argued that fear cannot be eliminated but only mastered, the next four Sections present *a second argument* that there are four ways to master fear. Dr. King's introduction ends with the question, "How may it be mastered?" And then, in the following four well-defined Sections, he answers this question.

> Section I. "First, we must unflinchingly face our fears and honestly ask ourselves why we are afraid."
> Section II. "Second, we can master fear through one of the supreme virtues known to man: courage."
> Section III. "Third, fear is mastered through love."
> Section IV. "Fear is mastered through faith."

6.9. Outline Section I. Your outline of Section I can easily follow Dr. King's text paragraph by paragraph.

6.10. Restate the argument of Section I.

Your outline of Section I of Dr. King's sermon is unlikely to clearly present his argument in that Section. That reflects an important point you encountered in *Reading*, namely, that argumentative texts for a mass audience usually do not follow a straight line of reasoning. To restate Dr. King's argument in Section I, you need to do some reworking of what he wrote and what you have outlined.

6.11. Outline Section II of this sermon.

6.12. Like most authors who write for, or speak to, the general public, Dr. King did not include in his sermon a sentence stating, "My thesis is . . ." or "I am going to prove that . . ." Nonetheless, his sermon does have a thesis, or two theses. What is his thesis, or what are his theses?

6.13. Does Dr. King's sermon state practical (action-guiding), theoretical (not action-guiding) arguments, or both?

If you think his arguments are theoretical, do they imply an unstated action-guiding statement or statements? Sermons, after all, generally are designed to motivate or to direct the members of a congregation to do something, like "Be generous to the poor . . ." If Dr. King is making only theoretical arguments, how is that consistent with this typical purpose of a sermon? If Dr. King intends his arguments to be theoretical, is his sermon more powerful by his leaving any further action-guiding conclusions unstated, leaving it up to his congregants to figure them out for themselves?

6.14. Outline each of the last two Sections of this sermon as we have done above. That exercise will allow you to understand (and appreciate the power of) the sermon in ways that you will never get from a quick read.

NOTES

1. Available at, https://time.com/5523797/united-states-russia-arms-treaty-trouble/.

2. Available at, https://www.africa.upenn.edu/Articles_Gen/Letter_Birmingham.html.

3. The complete essay is available at, https://theamericanscholar.org/the-disadvantages-of-an-elite-education/#.XkQa7Y3saQU.

4. Also available at, https://www.newsweek.com/ayanna-pressley-right-16-year-olds-deserve-right-vote-opinion-1469043.

Chapter 7

Ambiguity and Nonliteral Uses of Language

WHAT DO YOU KNOW?

Chapter 7 of *Reading* moved away from the "big picture" perspective of introductions, outlines, and summaries (which were the subjects of chapters 5 and 6), and focused on how an author's use of particular words, phrases, sentences, or longer passages creates, clarifies, or obscures her meaning. You learned that:

1. A word, phrase, sentence, or group of sentences is ambiguous when it (or they) can be reasonably interpreted in more than one way.

    a. *Semantic ambiguity* arises when there is more than one reasonable interpretation of a word or phrase.
    b. *Syntactic ambiguity* arises when the structure of a sentence or group of sentences creates more than one reasonable meaning for that sentence or group.

2. Factual sentences are distinct from normative sentences. Factual sentences refer to a state of affairs or condition in the world that can be proven true or false through one of your senses (sight, smell, etc.) or through scientific methods and tools. Normative sentences express or imply a norm (rule) or value, and often (but not always) express what a person or entity ought or should do.

3. Irony is the use of words to express a meaning that is the opposite of, or at least that markedly differs from, what the words literally mean. It is distinct from sarcasm.

4. Rhetoric is the use of language *to persuade* the reader or listener to act, to have a certain belief, or to have certain emotions, not through logical arguments (or not principally through these), but through appeals to the reader's (or listener's) emotions, feelings, or shared values, or to the character or reputation of the writer (or speaker).

EXERCISES

7.1. Let's return to Dr. King's essay, "Letter from a Birmingham Jail."[1]

 a. Consider this sentence: "We are caught in an inescapable network of mutuality, tied together in a single garment of destiny." (Paragraph 4)

 i. Is it ambiguous in any respect? If so, in what way?
 ii. Do the sentences immediately before and after this sentence provide any guidance as to what Dr. King means by it?

 b. Identify three ambiguous words, phrases, or sentences in this essay. State the reasonable meanings of each.
 c. Identify three or four of the most important rhetorical statements in the essay. (Hint: Is this sentence from paragraph 4 rhetorical or a statement of fact: "Injustice anywhere is a threat to justice everywhere"?)

 i. Does Dr. King attempt to argue in support of any of these statements? Or rather, does he assume that his readers will agree with these statements? Does he use them to support other claims he is making?

 d. Consider this highly rhetorical sentence from paragraph 13: "There comes a time when the cup of endurance runs over, and men are no longer willing to be plunged into the abyss of despair."

 i. Restate this as a declarative sentence. What meaning is lost in your restatement? Is any clarity gained? Any ambiguity removed?

 e. Consider this sentence: "We will win our freedom because the sacred heritage of our nation and the eternal will of God are embodied in our echoing demands." (It is in the middle of paragraph 35, a few paragraphs from the end of the essay; the paragraph starts "Perhaps I have once again been too optimistic.").

i. It is a beautiful sentence. What does it mean?
　　　ii. Is it consistent with Dr. King's rejection of "the myth of time" and his view that "Human progress never rolls in on wheels of inevitability; it comes through the tireless efforts and persistent work of men willing to be coworkers with God, and without this hard work time itself becomes an ally of the forces of stagnation" (paragraph 22)?

7.2. Re-read the essay "The Disadvantages of an Elite Education." An edited version is attached at Appendix C.[2]

　　a. Are any of the terms used in this essay ambiguous? Consider specifically whether "elite education" and "educational elite" are ambiguous. If not, why not?
　　b. If you think you have found one (or more) ambiguous terms, write down the various meanings of the term(s) as used by the author. How does the ambiguity affect the author's argument(s)?
　　c. Identify three or four rhetorical statements or passages in this essay. This exercise may be more difficult than, say, finding the rhetorical statements in Dr. King's "Letter from a Birmingham Jail," because the author is not obviously attempting to appeal to the reader's emotions or feelings through metaphors and imagery. Yet it does contain its own style of rhetoric and it is worth spending some time analyzing the text for its rhetoric.

7.3. The news media is full of articles and debates on how to reduce the greenhouse-gas emissions that cause climate change. One study has estimated that if the entire world adopted a vegan diet (giving up meat, dairy, and eggs), food-related emissions of greenhouse-gases could be cut by as much as 70%.[3] Because this is unlikely to happen in the near-term, if at all, some commentators have argued that abandoning wasteful organic farming and improving agricultural yields would be more likely to produce meaningful near-term reductions in greenhouse-gas emissions. To paraphrase one author's opinion, "Rather than false hopes about dietary change, real greenhouse-gas reductions require that the focus should be on improving agricultural practices."[4]

　　Is that a normative statement? If so, does it express a moral, legal, or some other type of value or norm?

7.4. Read the op-ed essay, "Who gets care for COVID-19 when hospitals fill up? Gut-wrenching decisions will have to be made."[5]

a. Identify all of the normative statements in the essay. Remember that not all normative statements contain an "ought," "should," "must," or the like.

b. Is the last sentence of the essay a normative statement?

7.5. Identify three normative statements in H.L. Mencken's essay on Grover Cleveland, "A Good Man in a Bad Trade."[6]

7.6. Go back to the op-ed piece on the true meaning of July 4, discussed in chapter 5 above and attached at Appendix D. Identify two rhetorical statements or passages in the text.

7.7. As we saw in chapter 4 of *Reading*, President Kennedy's inaugural address begins with this rhetorical sentence, "We observe today not a victory of party but a celebration of freedom—symbolizing an end as well as a beginning—signifying renewal as well as change." Restate the point(s) the President was trying to communicate in this sentence in a declarative, nonrhetorical sentence.

CASE STUDY: "ALL MEN ARE CREATED EQUAL"

In order to better understand the importance of spotting and analyzing ambiguous words, phrases, and sentences, we are going to walk through four possible interpretations of one part of one sentence of the *Declaration of Independence*. Specifically, we are going to analyze the phrase "all men are created equal" and four possible meanings it may have.

If you have never analyzed a text as we do in this case study, you may have to read through the following discussion several times to understand it. Do not be discouraged if you do. We all start our educations at different places. You have nothing to lose and much to gain. And you will get better in each subsequent effort.

Here is the first paragraph and part of the second paragraph of the *Declaration* to help place the phrase "all men are created equal" in context.

> When in the course of human events, it becomes necessary for one people to dissolve the political bands which have connected them with another, and to assume among the powers of the earth the separate and equal station to which the Laws of Nature and of Nature's God entitle them, a decent respect to the opinions of mankind requires that they should declare the causes which impel them to the separation.
>
> We hold these truths to be self-evident, that all men are created equal, that they are endowed by their Creator with certain unalienable rights, that among these are life, liberty, and the pursuit of happiness. That to secure these rights, governments are instituted among men, deriving their just powers from the consent of the governed. . . .

At this point, it would be helpful, but not necessary, for you to read the entire *Declaration* (it is not that long and it is profound in many ways).[7]

A complete reading of that text will make this case study easier to understand.

7.8. Let's start with a few simple questions to establish your current understanding of "all men are created equal."

a. When the *Declaration* says "all men are created equal," what does the author mean by that?[8] What thought did he intend to communicate by this phrase? Write down your best interpretation of this phrase.
b. Are there other meanings that this phrase could reasonably have? Is this phrase ambiguous in any way? Do your best to state two alternative meanings this phrase could have, in addition to the meaning you have already given this phrase.

Let's consider now four possible interpretations of this phrase, and in the course of our reviewing these, consider how your answers compare with each of them. Remember, the purpose of this discussion is not to propose or prove that any of these interpretations is the one and only "right" answer, although some are better than others. The discussion also does not suggest that these are the only reasonable interpretations of this phrase. If this were a book in American intellectual history, we might discuss one or two more interpretations. But adding them here would not advance your understanding of how to analyze ambiguities.

As we go through these four interpretations, recall the four conditions that constitute the "zone of reasonableness" (see chapter 3 of *Reading*) for an interpretation of an argumentative text. Do any of these four interpretations of "all men are created equal" violate one or more of those conditions? If so, that reading is not a very credible interpretation of what the author meant.

Interpretation #1. First, "all men are created equal" may mean that all men, as a matter of fact, are created equal in all respects. That is, it may mean that men are created equal in intelligence, musical and athletic ability, beauty, physical strength, moral qualities, opportunities in life, and so on.

Now, this is a possible interpretation of the phrase "all men are created equal" in large part because there is nothing in the *Declaration* that expressly contradicts this reading. The author of the *Declaration* did not go on to write, "and by this phrase I do not mean factually equal in all of their talents and traits, but rather I mean . . ."

So, while this is a possible interpretation, if you were to adopt this interpretation, what objections to it would you have to answer? The obvious one is that, interpreted in this way, this phrase is making a false statement. It is just factually false that you can play basketball as well as LeBron James or that he (or you or me) could have written Einstein's works on physics or painted as creatively as Van Gogh. Also, it is just a fact that some persons are born with severe mental or physical limitations, and others are not.

Moreover, in its social context, because many of the signers of the *Declaration* were slave holders, a condition that is inconsistent with a belief in the factual equality of all men, it is hard to believe that this is how they understood the sentence when they signed their names to the document. And, finally, this reading would have to address whether the signers meant "men" to be interpreted literally or whether they also meant it to include women. If they meant it to include women, did they believe that all men and women were factually equal in all respects? If so, why are there no women signers of the *Declaration*?

In short, it is hard to believe that the author of the *Declaration* or anyone who signed it was so oblivious to the factual differences between persons as to have this meaning. Nonetheless, this "all men are created equal in fact" reading is not contradicted by the express words of the text.

Interpretation #2. Consider this interpretation—that "all men are created equal" means something like, "all men have equal worth, equal dignity, equal human rights, or equal value." Maybe that is right, but where in the *Declaration* does it actually say any of those things? Does this reading import ideas into the *Declaration* that are not found there or, worse, that are 21st century concepts that were foreign to the author of the document?

In response, a proponent of this reading might say, "the very next clause in the sentence says, 'they are endowed by their Creator with certain unalienable rights' and so when we read 'all men are created equal' and this clause together, we see that the author meant that all men have equal rights." Well, maybe this is correct, but note how well does it fit with the actual text, what the document says?

If you think this response is correct, let's consider what you have to ignore. The sentence begins by saying we hold "these truths" (plural) to be self-evident, and then it goes on to enumerate the three truths—(1) all men are created equal, (2) all are endowed with unalienable rights, and (3) that among the unalienable rights are three specific rights, life, liberty, and the pursuit of happiness. (And note that the sentences that follow this one list still more self-evident truths.) So, the truth that all men are created equal is distinct from the second truth listed, namely, that all men have unalienable rights. Presumably, by listing these as separate truths, the author intended that they have independent meaning, that they refer to something different. That suggests that the idea of equality is not to be understood to be the same as the idea of unalienable rights and that the latter idea is not stated simply to give content to the former idea. To approach the point from another direction, the response and interpretation we are considering requires that we ignore the actual wording of the document and read it to mean something like, "there's one big self-evident truth and it is that all men have equal God-given rights and these include, at least, life, liberty, and the pursuit of happiness."

Now, why might this reading be the best reading, or at least not an unreasonable reading, even though you have to ignore what is actually in the text to get to it? Well, one reason relates to the political context of the document. (We discuss the importance of context in chapter 8 of *Reading*.) The *Declaration* is a political manifesto, a piece of political rhetoric, a document intended to build support for the Revolution in American public opinion and in the opinion of the international community ("a decent respect to the opinions of mankind," as stated in the first paragraph). It is not written as a precise philosophical text, where every statement and every clause are fine tuned to have the most precise meaning possible to establish a philosophical point or to fit in to some grand philosophical scheme. And when understood as such a document, it is a lot more rhetorically powerful to talk about many self-evident truths rather than just one, and it is better that they build on and reinforce each other so that it is harder to deny any one of them.

So, there is a good argument for the second interpretation. That interpretation has *some* affirmative support in the text itself and in its political context.

The point here is that if you are going to take it to be the "best" or "correct" reading, you need to understand what you are committing to, namely, to ignoring the actual words of the document and taking its purpose and the type of document it is as being more compelling reasons for that reading than are the actual, literal words of the text. You need to be self-conscious about your commitments in interpreting and understanding any text. Does being able to articulate this second interpretation mean that you understand the text, or specifically the phrase "all men are created equal"? Maybe. Are there alternatives that may make even better sense of the text?

Interpretation #3. Did you ever ask yourself why the *Declaration of Independence* is called a "declaration" rather than, say, *A Statement of the Causes for Our Separation from Great Britain,* or *The Reasons Why the Colonies Must Be Independent,* or something else along those lines?

By calling the document a "declaration," the author is trying to express the idea that this document is *not* primarily a *description* or *exposition* of facts, causes, or political principles. Rather, it is an *act* by which the colonies are making themselves a country independent of the mother country. Sometimes words are actions. "We hereby declare ourselves independent . . ." is like the bride and groom at a wedding saying, "I do." The bride and groom are not describing some facts in the world or taking some position on an issue. Rather, by their declaration "I do" the bride and groom are doing something—*marrying* each other. Similarly, by declaring themselves independent in this document, the colonists are *making* themselves independent.

Interpretations #1 and #2 of "all men are created equal" treat that phrase as *describing* the author's perceptions of men or as stating one of his political principles. The third interpretation treats this statement as part of a *declaration* of independence.

There's another way in which the term "declaration" tells us that the author and signers are *doing something* when they state "all men are created equal." When the author says that this is one of the truths "we hold to be self-evident" he is declaring that this principle is a fundamental principle for this new political community, that this is true because we colonists all publicly adopt it (declare it) as our governing first principle for this community. In this new democratic political order, we have all come together to declare ourselves members of a community in which each person is equal to every other, equal in rights and equal participants in our political life. It is solely by virtue of the political process that led to the creation of this document and its conclusion, this *Declaration*, that we are all equal.[9]

This reading is also not unreasonable. If the King of England, or anyone else, were to challenge the assertion that "all men are created equal" as factually or philosophically false, the author of the *Declaration* could simply respond, "The issue is not truth or falsity. We are telling the world what the rules of our community are (like the rules of a club), and this is the most important of them. If you want to belong to our new community (want to join the club), you need to accept this principle. If you do not like this rule, you can continue to live in a hierarchical society as you have done for years in England."

This interpretation reads the *Declaration* as the founding charter or document of an independent political body and *as an act stating the principles* of the community, regardless of whether anyone else in the world agrees or disagrees with those principles. The author is not trying to justify those principles by reference to anything other than the mere fact that the signers of the document agree to and adopt them. That is why the author can declare that they are "self-evident," because you are either in the club by adopting these principles or not, and no further justification is needed.

Given all of that analysis, does this reading ignore or gloss over any aspects of the text, what the author actually says? Or, worse, is it inconsistent with the actual words of the text? The first paragraph talks about "Laws of Nature" and "Nature's God," and the second paragraph references the "Creator." It sure looks like the author is trying to find a foundation for "all men are created equal" in religious teachings or a philosophical view of the world as being created by a God and following immutable natural laws which ground human rights. If this is correct, then "all men are created equal" is not just an arbitrary rule of the club, but rather is said to have a foundation in the Divine or Natural order of things. The first paragraph also mentions "a decent respect to the opinions of mankind . . ." Stating an arbitrary rule of the club hardly reflects such a "decent respect." Stating and adopting a rule which all (or most) of mankind would agree on because it is not arbitrary is a far better way of showing such respect.

In short, the third interpretation stresses one aspect of the *Declaration*—namely, that it is a declaration, a speech-act by which a new community comes into existence and gives voice to the most important rule of that community—at the expense of ignoring certain other words in the document. That does not make it a "bad" or "wrong" reading of the text, but if you think it is the correct interpretation, you need to recognize the limitations of and commitments made by it.

Interpretation #4. There is still another possible interpretation of "all men are created equal." This is the interpretation that President Lincoln may have been offering in the *Gettysburg Address*. Undoubtedly you recall that in the very first paragraph of that famous speech Lincoln stated that "our fathers" brought forth a new nation, "conceived in liberty, and dedicated to the proposition that all men are created equal." What did Lincoln mean by "dedicated to *the proposition* that all men are created equal . . ."?

One way to interpret this is that he is saying that the founding fathers, and the author of the *Declaration* in particular, understood the "self-evident" truth that "all men are created equal" to be like a scientific hypothesis, a statement or proposition that is to be tested to see if it is true. The founding fathers—especially people like Benjamin Franklin, Thomas Jefferson, Benjamin Rush, and others—were children of the Enlightenment and believed that the world of politics followed "Nature's Laws," just like the natural world does. They put forth the proposition that "all men are created equal" as a hypothesis to be tested, not in a science laboratory, but rather in a new political experiment, a new democratic political system. Lincoln's very next sentence in the *Gettysburg Address* supports this reading: "Now we are engaged in a great civil war, *testing* whether that nation, or any nation so conceived and so dedicated, can long endure." In other words, the Civil War was a continuation of the great experiment begun by the *Declaration* to determine whether an enduring political order can be based on the idea of the equality of all citizens.

Again, this is not an unreasonable reading of the *Declaration*. Like interpretation #2, it relies heavily on the context in which the document was written. So, how does it fit with the rest of the actual words of the *Declaration*?

Note how it does not rest easily with a critical term of the actual document—the term "self-evident." A self-evident truth is one that is so certain that it does not need to be tested or proven. It is not a possible truth. It is hardwired into us; we know it intuitively without any rational thought behind it (like $2 + 2 = 4$). So, a "self-evident" truth is not a hypothesis to be proven or a "proposition" that experience may prove to be true or false over time.

Beyond that, does this fourth interpretation make sense only in light of a speech delivered "fourscore and seven years" after the *Declaration*? Is this interpretation just an after-the-fact creation of Lincoln, or did the author of the *Declaration* really mean it? If he meant it, he could have said it, or could have said something like this, "no government in history has ever been founded on this principle, but we believe it can be the foundation of a new and better society, so we are embarking on this experiment for the betterment of all of our posterity . . ." The author of the *Declaration* would have been far more eloquent, of course, but you get the idea—there is nothing like that in the document. There is nothing tentative or uncertain in that text. Instead, the *Declaration* speaks with the voice of certainty, resolution, and firmness.

7.9. Compare the interpretation of "all men are created equal" that you wrote down before you read the four interpretations discussed above. Is your initial interpretation the same as or close to any of the four that we have considered in this case study?

7.10. What does your interpretation commit you to as far as ignoring or giving meaning to other parts of the text?

7.11. Are there broader political implications of your interpretation that do not flow from one of the other interpretations?

7.12. If you studied the history of the drafting of the *Declaration* and if you knew better the historical, political, or intellectual context of the document, do you think you would be more or less inclined to adopt one of these interpretations?

7.13. Read the entire *Declaration*. Does it make an argument(s)?

   a. For example, does it make any argument about the relation between "unalienable rights" and a just government? If so, what are the premises and conclusion of that argument?
   b. Does it make an argument about the legitimacy of the separation of the colonies from Great Britain? If so, what are the premises and conclusion of that argument?

7.14. The *Declaration* speaks of the right to "pursue happiness." If you were looking for an example of a broad, ambiguous term, you could not do much better than "happiness." Is there anything in the full text of the *Declaration* that fleshes out the idea of "pursuing happiness," that tells you what the author means by it? If not, what sources outside of the text could you go to for an answer to that question?

7.15. Consider this short passage on happiness, which is part of a speech that His Holiness the Dalai Lama gave to an audience in Arizona:

> I believe that the very purpose of our life is to seek happiness. That is clear. Whether one believes in religion or not, whether one believes in this religion or that religion, we are all seeking something better in life. So, I think, the very motion of our life is towards happiness . . .[10]

   a. Is this an argument?
   b. What are its premise (or premises) and conclusion?
   c. Analyze this passage along the lines of our analysis of the phrase "all men are created equal" from the *Declaration of Independence*.
   d. What does the Dalai Lama mean by "happiness"?
   e. Are there some definitions of the term that would tend to make his argument more internally consistent than others? For example, suppose "happiness" means having a life in which there is more pleasure than pain. Does that definition fit with the idea, found in the third sentence, of "seeking something better in life"?
   f. Later in the book in which the paragraph above is found, the Dalai Lama states that there are "four factors" of happiness—"wealth, worldly satisfaction, spirituality, and enlightenment."[11] How does that characterization of "happiness" affect the meaning of his argument?

7.16. In light of our discussion of irony in chapter 7 of *Reading*, is the phrase "all men are created equal" in the *Declaration of Independence* intended to be ironic? If you answered "no," why not?

The analysis we have undertaken of the phrase "all men are created equal" can, and should, be repeated with all texts that espouse moral or political views that include ambiguous or contentious terms. Engaging in such analysis is a matter of wrestling with terms and phrases we think we understand, or whose meaning we take for granted, or that are ambiguous, and trying to understand *what we are committing to* when we adopt or reject an interpretation of those terms or phrases.

This last statement is particularly important. We did not try to prove in this interpretative exercise that one of the four proposed readings is the "correct" one and the others are wrong. You can try to do that, of course. Before you go down that path, however, it is critical that you understand what any one reading commits you to with respect to the rest of the actual words of the text or other applicable standards (like common sense [we are not all equal in all of our capabilities] or the nature of the document in question [it is a political document and a declaration]). *Analysis is central to reading for understanding* because it reveals those commitments and allows us to weigh and judge them, and thus to arrive at better, richer understandings.

NOTES

1. Available at, https://www.africa.upenn.edu/Articles_Gen/Letter_Birmingham.html.

2. The complete essay is available at, https://theamericanscholar.org/the-disadvantages-of-an-elite-education/#.XkQa7Y3saQU.

3. *See, e.g.*, Bjorn Lomborg, "Vegetarianism as Climate Virtue Signaling," *Wall Street Journal*, p. A13, Aug. 9, 2019; also available at, https://www.wsj.com/articles/vegetarianism-as-climate-virtue-signaling-11565301932.

4. *Id.*

5. Available at, http://www.chicagotribune.com/opinion/commentary/ct-opinion-coronavirus-hospital-care-decisions-20200330-ci5h3kebfrdj7jlesnbqbgzpdq-story.html.

6. Available at, https://www.unz.com/print/AmMercury-1933jan-00125/.

7. Available at, https://www.archives.gov/founding-docs/declaration-transcript.

8. Thomas Jefferson was the principal author of the *Declaration*. His initial draft was revised and edited by a committee that included four other persons. For simplicity, I will just refer to "the author" of the document.

9. This interpretation of the phrase owes much to Charles L. Mee, Jr., *A Visit to Haldeman and Other States of Mind*, pp. 163–64 (Lanham, MD: M. Evans 2014).

10. His Holiness the Dalai Lama and Howard C. Cutler, M.D., *The Art of Happiness*, p. 13 (London: Hodder & Stoughton 2009).

11. *Id.*, p. 24.

Chapter 8

Context Imparts Meaning

WHAT DO YOU KNOW?

In chapter 8 of *Reading* we examined how five types of context can impart meaning to a text.

1. The intellectual context of a text is the dialogue or debate in which the text is participating; this dialogue or debate is made up of the arguments, theses, questions, or problems asserted by other writers, whether historical or contemporaneous with the author. The first, but not the only, place to look for the intellectual context of an argumentative text is within the text itself.
2. The social, political, and cultural contexts of a text refer to the social, political, or cultural circumstances in which a text is written. When an author expressly or implicitly refers to the social, political, or cultural circumstances in which a text is written, he generally does so to import into the text the meanings that the audience associates with those circumstances. Those circumstances may be historical or contemporaneous with the text. In addition, a reader may refer to the social, political, and cultural contexts of a text to give it meaning even when an author does not expressly refer to such contexts.
3. Physical context refers to an author's expressed or implied beliefs about the physical environment of her subjects. While physical context is not important for understanding many types of argumentative texts (*e.g.*, a philosophical essay on logic or ethics), some argumentative texts will require you to understand physical context to determine what the author means.

EXERCISES

8.1. Go back to the op-ed piece on the true meaning of July 4th, discussed in chapter 5 above and attached at Appendix D. What is the intellectual or cultural context for the text? In answering this question, note that the author relies on both historical evidence and contemporaneous events (*e.g.*, barbeques, fireworks) to make his argument.

8.2. Re-read the *Gettysburg Address*, which we discussed in chapter 4 above. Do any parts of this text rely on context to add meaning to the argument? If so, what kind of context?

8.3. Recall our discussion in chapter 6 in *Reading* of the essay on lowering the voting age, "Ayanna Pressley Is Right: 16-Year-Olds Deserve the Right to Vote," attached at Appendix B of *Reading*.

 a. The second paragraph of the essay is one-sentence. It begins, "This imperative is front and center . . ." I did not include this sentence in my outline of the essay or in my restatements of the author's argument. Is it essential to the author's argument? In other words, does she need this sentence as a premise in order to reach her conclusion? Can she reach her conclusion (without any logical error) if this sentence is not included as a premise?
 b. If you (like me) also did not include it in your outline or restatement, why not?
 c. Does this sentence provide context for the author's argument?
 d. Does it have any rhetorical effect?

8.4. Take another look at Dr. King's "Letter from a Birmingham Jail."[1] This is a good example of a nonacademic essay in which the author makes clear both the intellectual context (*i.e.*, the dialogue) which his essay is part of, and the social and cultural context of the issues and events discussed in that essay. We discussed the intellectual context of this essay in chapter 8 of *Reading*.

 a. State in a sentence or two the social and cultural context in which the essay was written.
 b. Dr. King's discussion of just and unjust laws (paragraphs 13 through 19) is somewhat philosophical.

  i. Would more knowledge of the events leading to Dr. King's arrest help you understand those passages? Would more knowledge of the issues facing Dr. King's nonviolent protests or the civil rights movement at the time of the essay assist your understanding?

ii. Go to a secondary source that discusses Dr. King's activities prior to the writing of his Letter. Then come back and re-read these passages. How does that new knowledge of context add to your understanding of these passages?

CASE STUDY: AN OPINION PIECE ON FEDERAL MARIJUANA REGULATION

Debates about the regulation, deregulation, criminalization, and decriminalization of various drugs have long historical roots in this country. The political battle to ban the sale of alcohol (prohibition) began in earnest around the middle of the 19th century. That battle effectively ended after nearly a century with the repeal of the 18th amendment to the Constitution in 1933 and the regulation of alcohol by the states.

The recent passage of state laws that decriminalize the sale and possession of marijuana for medical or recreational purposes, and the proposals to pass such laws in other states, have taken place against a backdrop of federal law in which marijuana is still regulated as a dangerous drug, a so-called Schedule I drug under the federal Controlled Substances Act. Since at least the late 1960s, there has been a vigorous, even if periodic, debate over whether the federal government should stop regulating marijuana in any fashion.

With that background in mind, read the opinion piece, "It's Time to End Any Level of Federal Marijuana Prohibition," attached at Appendix F.[2]

8.5. This is an argumentative text, as is indicated by the title of the essay, for example.

a. So, we know the essay will have a thesis. State the thesis. If you think the article has more than one statement of its thesis, identify all of them.
b. What type of argument does this article make?

8.6. What does the structure of the text tell us about what the author intends to communicate?

You know that our approach to reading is flexible and practical. So, instead of doing a detailed outline of this essay as we did with other texts in chapter 6 of *Reading,* suppose you were to do a very general outline. That would nicely illustrate the structure of this text as a whole. It will be most useful if your outline focuses both on what the author is doing and the particulars of what he is saying. This is the start of such a generic outline:

48   *Chapter 8*

   1. Paragraph 1: The author writes about current legislative proposals to reform federal marijuana laws and states a thesis.
   2. Paragraphs 2–3: _____
   3. Paragraphs 4–7 (first part): _____
   4. Beginning of paragraph 7: _____
   5. Last few sentences of paragraph 7: _____
   6. Paragraphs 8–9: _____

If this is confusing at first glance (especially with respect to paragraph 7), focus on how the author uses the similarities and dissimilarities of alcohol and other drugs to prove his thesis (or theses) in paragraphs 1 through 7. In paragraphs 8 through 10, the argument does not rest on similarities or dissimilarities. Note that the author employs different types of evidence to make his point in these last three paragraphs.

   8.7. In paragraph 4 through the beginning of paragraph 7, the author expressly argues by analogy—the analogy between alcohol and marijuana. You know from chapter 4 of *Reading* that reasoning by analogy is one type of inductive reasoning.

It will be useful to take a closer look at reasoning by analogy. You intuitively already know what reasoning by analogy involves, since we do it all the time. This discussion will give your knowledge a bit more focus.

The general form of reasoning by analogy is:

> A is like (or is similar to) B because both have characteristics 1, 2, 3 (maybe more or fewer).
> A also has characteristic 4.
> Therefore, B likely has characteristic 4.

The more properties that A and B share, the more likely it is that they also share some other, additional property. The fewer properties they share, the less likely that they will share an additional property. To quote the Scottish philosopher David Hume (1711–1786), "The liker the better," *i.e.,* the more A and B are alike, the stronger the reasoning from the known properties of both A and B to the unknown properties of B.

When you see this form of argument, ask yourself: (1) in what respects are A and B alike, (2) are those similarities relevant to prove the conclusion they are offered to prove, (3) are there relevant dissimilarities between A and B that undermine the conclusion the author is asking us to draw about B, and (4) even if there are no known relevant dissimilarities, do the similarities require that I accept what the author says about B? All of this is fairly abstract. A few examples will help put meat on these bones.

Consider this example:

Dogs are mammals, can do tricks, and have four legs.
Killer whales are mammals and can do tricks.
Therefore, killer whales likely have four legs.

Is this inductive argument by analogy strong or weak? One relevant dissimilarity between dogs and killer whales shows the analogy to be flawed and the inductive reasoning to be weak. What is it? Obviously, it is that one animal lives on land and one lives in water.

Let's look at another example:

On earth, scientists have found some form of life every place where there is oxygen, water, and moderate temperatures.
Scientists have found a planet, AlphaBetaSoupa, in another solar system which has oxygen, water, and moderate temperatures.
So, there is probably life on planet AlphaBetaSoupa.

In this second example, the analogy (and the inductive argument) is strong if oxygen, water, and moderate temperatures are all that is needed for life to exist (if they are sufficient for life to exist).

But suppose they are not all that is needed. Suppose life also requires an atmosphere that blocks out extreme radiation from the planet's sun, relatively little poisonous gas in the atmosphere, and other conditions. If that were the case, then the analogy (and the inductive argument) is weaker, because the argument does not tell us whether AlphaBetaSoupa is similar to earth in having these other conditions.

With this discussion in mind, is the author's analogy between alcohol and marijuana a strong or weak inductive argument? If you are not sure, what additional types of facts would you need to know to answer that question?

> 8.8. This essay is particularly interesting in that the author also argues by dis-analogy, that is, by pointing out the dissimilarities between marijuana and other drugs (especially in paragraphs 2 and 3). Is the author's argument about the dissimilarities between marijuana and the other Schedule I drugs a strong or weak inductive argument? If you are not sure, what additional types of facts would you need to know to answer that question?
>
> 8.9. Is the author's argument in paragraph 8 against rescheduling marijuana (taking it out of Schedule I and placing it into a lower Schedule) strong or weak? If you are not sure, what additional types of facts would you need to know to answer that question?
>
> 8.10. Answer these questions on contexts:
>
> > a. What is the context for this text?
> > b. Does that context add any meaning to the text?

c. The author is arguing for the federal deregulation of marijuana. Through his analogy to alcohol, he is suggesting that marijuana regulation should be left to the states (see especially paragraph 6). In light of that, is there any context that you expected to find here that is not here? How would that context strengthen the author's argument, if at all?

CASE STUDY FOR EXPERTS: A BOOK REVIEW BY H.L. MENCKEN

This case study is called a "Case Study for Experts" and is the last one in this *Workbook* because it is perhaps the most difficult one. Nonetheless, there is much to be learned from going through it. It is difficult, but now you have the tools to do it. *You can do it.*

H.L. Mencken was a controversial and sometimes bombastic essayist, critic, and newspaper columnist from the early 1900s through the 1940s. He was highly influential because of the breadth of his knowledge and opinions, and because he wrote at a time when most Americans got their news and opinions from newspapers and magazines.

In this case study, we analyze Mencken's review of a biography of President Grover Cleveland. Read "A Good Man in a Bad Trade."[3]

This essay is difficult to analyze, in part because it is written in a style that is now out-of-date and because of its loose treatment of several related concepts. That makes it particularly appropriate for the last of our case studies.

8.11. Outline the essay and state its thesis, as we have done with other texts. The fact that this essay is a book review should not alter in any significant way how you analyze the text, and specifically how you do your outline.

You have done your outline of this essay and restatement of its thesis. (You could continue reading this case study if you have not completed these tasks, but you will learn a lot less if you do.) As we did with other essays, let's start our discussion with my outline.

Outline

1. At least since George Washington, the United States has not had a president whose fundamental character was more solid or more admirable than President Cleveland's. [Paragraph 1, second sentence, paraphrased]

2. Presidents who are widely regarded as great, such as Lincoln, Theodore Roosevelt, and Woodrow Wilson, appear pliant, irresolute, and to have been manipulated by others ("worked by strings"), compared to Cleveland. [Paragraph 1]
3. Cleveland had no "strings" attached. [Paragraph 1]
4. Cleveland defied politicians and the general public when they opposed his "sound and honest" decisions, rather than yielding to them. [Paragraph 1]
5. Cleveland was more "self-sufficient" than any other man in modern history. [Paragraph 1]
    a. Once he made up his mind, "he stood immovable," even when he was bitterly hated. [Paragraph 1]
    b. He came into and left office without compromising his character. [Paragraph 1]
6. Cleveland's "steadfastness" was not a function of his physical size, but of his character. [Paragraph 2]
    a. There was "no give in him, no bounce, no softness." [Paragraph 2]
7. His youth had been hard and he learned little of the "spiritual" (*i.e.*, cultural) heritage of man. [Paragraph 3]
    a. He remained somewhat stodgy and pedantic all of his life. [Paragraph 3]
    b. He admired "solid men" like himself. [Paragraph 3]
    c. His lack of cultural refinement led him to be influenced by average men and, specifically, by his Secretary of State, a defective statesman, into blunders in domestic (the Pullman strike) and foreign (the Venezuelan message) affairs. [Paragraph 4]
8. Once Cleveland made up his mind, he stuck to his course, even when that course was in error. [Paragraph 4]
9. Cleveland was principally motivated by a sense of duty that was an outgrowth of his Calvinistic beliefs. [Paragraph 5]
10. It is unlikely that we shall see a president or politician with Cleveland's virtues again. [Paragraph 6]
    a. Politicians today are flexible and quick to compromise. [Paragraph 6]
    b. In today's politics, frankness and courage are luxuries of the political losers. [Paragraph 6]
11. One of the problems with America today is that Cleveland's character is not taught in textbooks, and he is relegated to a place in history below other, more famous politicians. [Paragraph 6, last four sentences]
12. This is an excellent biography, competently written and showing understanding and discretion. [Paragraph 7]

One reason why your outline of this essay may differ from this outline relates to the style of the essay. The essay consists of seven long paragraphs. That is not the style for current essays in the mass media. If the essay were written today, the author or his editor probably would have broken each of those long paragraphs into several shorter ones. As the outline above illustrates, most of these long paragraphs incorporate multiple thoughts. Moreover, most of the principal points of the essay are found in the midst of these paragraphs, not at the beginning or end of them. Because I read Mencken as arguing for a thesis about President Cleveland, my outline selects the sentences that are most closely related to the thesis, except for the last two paragraphs, which I do not view as stating premises that support the thesis.

The Thesis. Some book reviews are no more than a recitation of the nature and contents of the book being reviewed with some criticism or praise for the book added to the mix. In contrast, Mencken's book review says relatively little about the book being reviewed and a lot about the subject of the book, namely, President Cleveland. Moreover, Mencken uses this review to make an argument about the character of that subject.

So, what is Mencken's thesis? Does he state it clearly, or did you have to engage in a major rephrasing of his words to state it coherently?

As I read the essay, the thesis is in the second sentence of the essay, and stated in number 1 of the outline. To rephrase that sentence, his thesis is: "at least since George Washington, the United States has not had a President whose fundamental character was more solid or more admirable than President Cleveland's." Note that this sentence is not action-guiding for anyone; it does not tell anyone to do anything. This is a theoretical argument, as we used that term in chapter 1 of *Reading*.

Your immediate reaction to this thesis may be that it is false, or at least too strong. If you took the standard high school history courses, you learned that there are many other presidents who are more admired for their character than Cleveland. Lincoln, for example, is commonly remembered as "Honest Abe." Very few people (maybe no one) remember President Cleveland, if they know of him at all, as "Honest Grover." Because of George Washington's reputation for integrity, the myth arose that when his father asked if he chopped down the cherry tree, he replied, "I cannot tell a lie." There is no widely circulated anecdote of Cleveland's rectitude that puts him on the same moral plane as Washington.

Before you commit to the view that the thesis is false, you will find it profitable to ask yourself, what does it mean? The truth or falsity of Mencken's thesis depends in large measure on what he means by two broad and ambiguous terms in that thesis—"solid" and "admirable." These terms imply value judgments or ethical rules. (Such statements are called *normative statements* and are distinguished from purely factual statements, like "eating an additional 5 grams of fiber daily will make you healthier." See chapter 7 of

Reading.) When Mencken uses these terms, is he referring to virtues such as honesty, generosity, loyalty, truthfulness, or something else?

To say that "X is a solid fellow" often means something like "X is a trustworthy (or honest) fellow." That is to make a statement about X's virtues or ethical character. But "solid," when used by Mencken in this essay, may mean that X is inflexible, uncompromising, rigid, unwilling to consider other viewpoints, or dogmatic. "Admirable" is also vague. X may be an admirable scientist because he pursues the truth in his field of study at all costs, but X otherwise may be a terrible person, because he is mean to little kids, cheats everyone he can, and so on. What does it mean to be an "admirable" politician or president?

The point is: *when you encounter a statement that uses ambiguous terms, your task is to dig into the text to discover what the author means by those terms.* You may find, as in this essay, that the structure of a text provides insights into the meaning of those terms, including its ambiguous terms. Specifically, here, outlining Mencken's essay can reveal both the meaning of the thesis and the premises the author uses to prove the thesis. If you never outlined this essay, you may have hastily concluded that number 7 in the outline is irrelevant to or inconsistent with his thesis, rather than seeing that it may play a vital role in illustrating what Mencken means by his thesis, and particularly what he means by "solid" and "admirable."

> 8.12. What does the outline above show us about the relationship of the statements and evidence offered in the essay? To begin, notice that each statement in numbers 2 through 9 in the outline (ignoring the subpoints) is intended to be independent of the others, is offered to support the thesis of the essay, and is not offered to support (is not evidence for) any of the other points in the essay.

Let's focus on numbers 5, 6, 7, and 10 in the outline and the subpoints that are offered to support the propositions stated in those numbers. What is the relationship between those numbers and the subpoints under each of them?

> 8.13. What is the logical relationship between Mencken's thesis and numbers 2 through 5 (including subpoints 5.a and 5.b) in the outline? Do these statements support that thesis, contradict it, or are they not relevant to it? For your convenience, those parts of the outline are:
>
> > 2. Presidents who are widely regarded as great, such as Lincoln, Theodore Roosevelt, and Woodrow Wilson, appear pliant, irresolute, and to have been manipulated by others ("worked by strings"), compared to Cleveland. [Paragraph 1]
> > 3. Cleveland had no "strings" attached. [Paragraph 1]

4. Cleveland defied politicians and the general public when they opposed his "sound and honest" decisions, rather than yielding to them. [Paragraph 1]
5. Cleveland was more "self-sufficient" than any other man in modern history. [Paragraph 1]
   a. Once he made up his mind, "he stood immovable," even when he was bitterly hated. [Paragraph 1]
   b. He came into and left office without compromising his character. [Paragraph 1]

8.14. Focus more closely on number 7 in the outline and the subpoints under it:

7. His youth had been hard and he learned little of the "spiritual" (*i.e.*, cultural) heritage of man. [Paragraph 3]
   a. He remained somewhat stodgy and pedantic all of his life. [Paragraph 3]
   b. He admired "solid men" like himself. [Paragraph 3]
   c. His lack of cultural refinement led him to be influenced by average men and, specifically, by his Secretary of State, a defective statesman, into blunders in domestic (the Pullman strike) and foreign (the Venezuelan message) affairs. [Paragraph 4]

How does number 7, and its subpoints, support Mencken's thesis, if they do? A lot of people have "hard" childhoods and are not exposed to the "higher" forms of culture (art, music, and literature), and turn out to be scoundrels, petty criminals, or serial killers. They are not "solid" or "admirable" persons. Are these statements of little or no relevance in supporting Mencken's thesis? Are they completely irrelevant to the thesis or inconsistent with it?

8.15. The last three numbers in the outline reflect statements that are not clearly part of Mencken's argument. Recall that they are:

10. It is unlikely that we shall see a president or politician with Cleveland's virtues again. [Paragraph 6]
    a. Politicians today are flexible and quick to compromise. [Paragraph 6]
    b. In today's politics, frankness and courage are luxuries of the political losers. [Paragraph 6]
11. One of the problems with America today is that Cleveland's character is not taught in textbooks, and he is relegated to a place in history below other, more famous politicians. [Paragraph 6, last four sentences]

> 12. This is an excellent biography, competently written and showing understanding and discretion. [Paragraph 7]

Number 10 summarizes the parts of paragraph 6 commenting on the then-current political culture. Is this restatement (a) intended to support the thesis, (b) a conclusion to be drawn from the argument, or (c) not part of and not implied by the argument?

> 8.16. Number 11 in the outline (summarizing the last four sentences of paragraph 6) does not support the thesis. The thesis is about Cleveland's character. These last four sentences do not provide additional evidence that Cleveland's character was "solid" or "admirable." Instead, they can reasonably be interpreted to state to the reader, "you would know what I am telling you about Cleveland if the education you received weren't so bad, if teaching history to schoolchildren was more than a 'puerile racket'."

This is an example of a text including statements that are not strictly speaking part of the argument, but that are included because the author apparently believes they support the thesis indirectly by making a related but independent point or because they are intended to have rhetorical impact. Mencken offers no support for his criticism of American education. Moreover, he does not take the fact that Cleveland's character is not taught in the schools as evidence that his thesis about Cleveland's character is wrong. Rather, he appears to be taking the position, "I am right about Cleveland; this truth about Cleveland's character is not widely known because our educational system is poor (a "puerile racket")." Needless to say, that is a strong position to take without any argument. That sort of approach—"I'm the pundit and I'm here to pronounce my opinions, with supporting evidence or not"—is not uncommon in essays in the mass media. Outlining an argumentative text allows you to more readily distinguish those sorts of conclusory statements ("If I say it, it must be true") from those that are part of the argument and supported by some sort of evidence.

Number 12 in the outline (summarizing paragraph 7 of Mencken's article) also is not a statement of or relevant to proving Mencken's thesis. Its connection to Mencken's thesis and premises is even more distant than the last four sentences of paragraph 6. So why is it in the outline?

> 8.17. From the preceding discussion and questions, you are in a position to take the major points of Mencken's essay and restate them into his argument, omitting the points that are not part of his argument. Give it a try, recognizing that it may be difficult given the way Mencken has written this essay, especially paragraph 1.

Do a very general and then a more detailed reconstruction of Mencken's argument. If you are having trouble getting started, you already know what his thesis is, so you can make that the conclusion of the argument, and then the other points would precede that. Those other points would include at least some form of numbers 2 through 9 of the outline.

8.18. Does the social, political, or cultural context of Mencken's essay assist your analysis of its meaning? Here is a very brief summary of its political and social context. This essay was published about a decade after the infamous Teapot Dome scandal of the Harding administration, after the economic boom and bust of the 1920s, after the first election of Franklin D. Roosevelt to the Presidency (but before Roosevelt assumed office), and more than three years into the Great Depression.

If this brief summary is of little or no assistance in analyzing this essay, what additional context may assist, if any? Is this an essay that stands on its own and for which context adds little to no additional meaning?

Note that none of the preceding analysis of Mencken's essay has been critical of his thesis or the evidence he presents in support of that thesis. We are trying to understand the point Mencken is making (what does he [claim] to know and how does he [claim] to know it) *before* we consider where that argument may fall short or go astray, if it does. Use your critical reaction as a jumping-off point to further analysis and a better understanding of the text. When you have gone as far as you can in using your criticisms to understand a text, then you can assess the merits of the argument.

If you were inclined to criticize the essay in order to do a deeper dive into its meaning, to understand it better, you could approach it from any one of three critical perspectives:

- From a historical perspective, you may want to know more about Cleveland and his two presidential terms in order to assess whether Mencken has omitted any contrary evidence on Cleveland's character.
- From an ethical perspective, you could ask whether Mencken's ethical views are adequate. Can the traits he finds to be "solid" and "admirable" also be interpreted as inflexibility, stubbornness, brashly and imprudently failing to heed consequences, and so on?
- If your answer to this question is affirmative, you may also consider a political criticism, namely, are these desirable qualities in a politician, leader, or president?

Pursuing any of these possible critical lines of inquiry may lead to greater understanding of the strengths and weaknesses of the thesis and argument of this essay.

NOTES

1. Available at, https://www.africa.upenn.edu/Articles_Gen/Letter_Birmingham.html.

2. Also available at It's Time to End Any Level of Federal Marijuana Prohibition | Cato Institute.

3. Available at, https://www.unz.com/print/AmMercury-1933jan-00125/.

Chapter 9

The ABCs of Logic

WHAT DO YOU KNOW?

In chapter 9 of *Reading*, we dipped our toes into the deep sea of logic. Specifically, we learned:

1. A fallacy is a common error in reasoning.
2. *Equivocation* (*ambiguity*) occurs when the author (or speaker) gives a critical word or phrase in the premises of an argument two different meanings and draws a conclusion from those premises that is possible only because of the ambiguity in the critical term or phrase.
3. *Begging the question* (*or circular reasoning*) refers to the fallacy that occurs when the premises assume the conclusion (the question) that those premises are trying to prove. When you beg the question, you are arguing in a circle, because the premises do not provide independent proof of a conclusion, but rather assume the conclusion that is to be proven (often by restating it in other words).
4. *Non sequitur* ("*that which does not follow*") is the logical fallacy of drawing a conclusion from a premise or premises that are irrelevant to the conclusion, that provide no support for the conclusion.
5. The *ad hominem* (literally, *directed to the man*) fallacy is committed when the author (or speaker) either (a) attacks the person making an argument rather than attacking the premises of that argument or (b) appeals to the listener's special circumstances as a ground for accepting or rejecting the writer's (speaker's) conclusion, rather than supporting that conclusion with reasons any person could accept.

6. Arguments committing the fallacy of *ignorance* argue either that some statement is true because no one has ever proven it to be false or that some statement is false because it has not been proven to be true.
7. To say that Y is a necessary condition of X is to say that the truth of Y is necessary for X to be true. X cannot be true if Y is false.
8. To say that X is a sufficient condition of Y is to say that the truth of X is sufficient (all that you need) for Y to be true. If X is true, then Y cannot be false.

EXERCISES

9.1. Identify the type of fallacy found in each of these arguments:

  a. Mr. Hall is a pain in the neck. At every school board meeting he complains about how badly our students are being taught. I don't care what his data shows about the lack of math proficiency in our 8th grade students. He's a wrongheaded gadfly.
  b. Our entire human existence is suffering, more suffering, and then death. As an English writer once said, "man is born, he suffers, and then dies." We can conclude that happiness is an illusion.
  c. Politician: The president's foreign policy has made the world less safe; it's a disaster. His domestic policy has left millions unemployed, created high inflation, and is terrible for the working class. He's the poorest president we have ever had.
  Constituent: He's worth a billion dollars, so I don't see how he can be our poorest president.
  d. The First Amendment to the Constitution guarantees freedom of speech. Shouting "fire" in a crowded theater is protected free speech under the Constitution. Therefore, we all have a Constitutional right to shout "fire" in a crowded theater.
  e. We know that the United States didn't land on the moon in 1969. All those astronauts-on-the-moon photos are fake. No one has ever proven that the moon landing was real.
  f. Our enemies are innovative and resourceful, and so are we. They never stop thinking about ways to harm our country, and neither do we. (President George W. Bush)
  g. Lee Harvey Oswald was part of a conspiracy to kill President Kennedy. He couldn't have done it alone. So, there must have been others who conspired with him.
  h. Political candidate to reporter: Senator X is a lying liar. So, rather than asking me why I changed my position on climate change, why don't you try to get the truth out of him on that issue?

i. Of course I'm telling you the truth. I go to church every Sunday.
j. How do I know Smith is a thief? I saw him walking a dog with my binoculars.
k. In paragraph 6 of his essay on President Cleveland, Mencken writes: "If pedagogy were anything save the puerile racket that it is, he [Cleveland] would loom large in the textbooks."

9.2. Identify the necessary and sufficient conditions, if any, in the following examples. If you believe that a sentence does not state a necessary or sufficient condition, state the reasons why you think that.

a. You can't live without water.
b. You can live a few weeks without food.
c. Human life only needs water, food, and oxygen to survive.
d. If John is an unmarried man, then he is a bachelor.
e. If John is a bachelor, he is an unmarried man.
f. If Mary is the smartest student in the class, then she is smart.
g. I'll pay your tuition next semester, but only if you get a job to pay for books.
h. Ian is John's son. So, John is a father.
i. Ian is Beatrice's son only if Beatrice is Ian's mother.
j. Dinosaurs didn't read. Now they're extinct. (https://www.grammarly.com/blog/jokes-to-warm-your-bookish-heart/)

9.3. Suppose you read this in a newspaper editorial:

> The most thoughtful politicians know that breaking up the concentration of wealth and economic power of corporations, even though indispensable, would not by itself produce widespread prosperity.

Is the author stating a necessary condition, sufficient condition, or neither?

9.4. Consider this sentence from Dr. King's "Letter from a Birmingham Jail" (paragraph 15):

> A law is unjust if it is inflicted on a minority that, as a result of being denied the right to vote, had no part in enacting or devising the law.

What is the sufficient condition stated? The necessary condition? If you are uncertain, how would you restate this sentence as an "If X, then Y" statement?

9.5. Consider another example from Dr. King's "Letter from a Birmingham Jail" (paragraph 11):

> My friends, I must say to you that we have not made a single gain in civil rights without determined legal and nonviolent pressure.

Eliminating the introductory phrases, this substance of the sentence is:

> We have not made a single gain in civil rights without determined legal and nonviolent pressure.

Does this sentence state a necessary condition? A sufficient condition?

9.6. Consider this quote:

> Action may not always bring happiness, but there is no happiness without action. (attributed to Benjamin Disraeli, British politician and statesman, 1804–1881)

What is Disraeli saying about action being either a necessary or sufficient condition of happiness?

9.7. Does this sentence state a necessary or sufficient condition, neither, or both:

> We cannot achieve social justice until we achieve equality of opportunity.

9.8. Does this sentence state a necessary or sufficient condition, neither, or both:

> If you want peace, work for justice.

9.9. Consider this statement:

> If the leaders of the superpowers want to kill 100 million people in an hour, then all they need to do is start a nuclear war.

Does this state a necessary condition, sufficient condition, neither, or both?

EXERCISES FOR EXTRA STUDY

If you find that your enthusiasm for necessary and sufficient conditions is running low on fuel, you can stop reading here, declare victory, and go for a cup of coffee or a run. But if your enthusiasm is just getting warmed up and you have not had nearly enough of these concepts, this section is for you. Keep reading and have fun.

In many of the articles and texts you read, authors will not use the "if . . . , then . . . ," "only if," or similar phrasing to state necessary or sufficient conditions. Their writing would be boring if they did this all the time. So, in this section we will look at some examples in common usage and try to figure out which terms state the necessary and sufficient conditions, if any.

9.10. How would you restate this sentence as an "if . . . , then . . ." statement to make clear the speaker's intent?

>All we need to solve the opioid crisis is for everyone under 40 to have a good, meaningful job.

9.11. When you see the word "need," you have a red flag that what follows is a statement of a necessary condition.

    a. How would you paraphrase this paragraph as an "if . . . , then . . ." or "only if" statement?

>People often ask me whether there is any one thing we need to live a moral life. Spiritual teachers and religious traditions over the years have answered this question in many ways, of course. I think the answer is recognizing that we are all fundamentally interconnected.

    b. What is the necessary condition expressed by your restatement?
    c. The sufficient condition?

9.12. When you see the word "requirement" (or "requirements") you have a red flag that what follows is a necessary condition. So, how would you restate this sentence to make clear the necessary condition(s)?

>To be stupid, selfish, and have good health are three requirements for happiness . . . (Gustave Flaubert, French novelist, in a letter to Madame Louise Colet, August 1846)

9.13. Lets's go fishing for a sufficient condition:

    a. Does this paragraph state a sufficient condition? If so, what is it?

>Stanley says that catching big fish depends on many different factors—water temperature, the type of equipment you use, your lures, and how you present your lures to the fish, among many others. But I disagree. I think that on any day that it is cloudy but not raining, you will catch big fish.

    b. What are the author's views on catching big fish when it is cloudy and it is raining?

9.14. Consider this sentence:
All men and women are brothers and sisters, and until we recognize that we will never have peace on earth.

    a. How would you rephrase this sentence to interpret it as stating a necessary condition?
    b. Recall what we learned about ambiguous terms in chapter 7 of *Reading*. The sentence immediately above is packed with

ambiguities. "We" is ambiguous. "Peace on earth" is ambiguous. "All men and women are brothers and sisters" is ambiguous (and rhetorical, since it is literally false).

What does "we" mean in this sentence? Write down two or three possible meanings. What are the implications of each of those meanings for there being peace on earth?

c. Do the same sort of analysis of the ambiguous terms "peace on earth" and "all men and women are brothers and sisters."

9.15. This is a quote from a book on Buddhism:

Without suffering, you cannot grow.[1]

The statement is saying that suffering (or having suffered) is a necessary condition of growing. (Given its source, assume that "growing" means "growing spiritually.") How would you rephrase this as an "if . . . , then . . ." statement?

9.16. Do any of these statements express a necessary or sufficient condition?

Depression is a form of mental illness that afflicts many artists, actors, politicians, and intellectuals. Abraham Lincoln and Winston Churchill both suffered from depression. So did the great painter Van Gogh, the musical genius Mozart, and the novelist Ernest Hemingway. Depression knows no economic or social boundaries and is not limited to a particular field of endeavor.

9.17. Does this passage say that concentration is a necessary condition of being a better reader, a sufficient condition, or neither?

Concentration is hardly the only element in becoming a better reader. It is essential to being a better reader, but far from adequate by itself.

9.18. Suppose you are in the Pacific Northwest. Your friend says:

If it's not raining, then we're not in Seattle.

Seattle, of course, is notorious for its many days and months of rainy weather. So, what is your friend saying here in terms of necessary or sufficient conditions?

EXTRA EXERCISES FOR EXPERTS: TWO ARGUMENT FORMS AND TWO RELATED FALLACIES

If you are really enthusiastic about the distinction between necessary and sufficient conditions (and who wouldn't be?), you will want to know about

The ABCs of Logic

two common types of argument that more formally exhibit these concepts, and two related fallacies that exhibit the incorrect use of them.

Modus ponens is a form of deductive argument with this simple structure:

If X, then Y.
X.
Therefore, Y.

For example:
If you want to eat something for better health, eat more fiber.
You want to eat something for better health.
So, eat more fiber (or, you should eat more fiber).
Or,
If we're in Seattle, then it's raining.
We're in Seattle.
Therefore, it's raining.
Or,
If we want to create widespread prosperity, then we must break up the concentration of wealth and power.
We want widespread prosperity.
We conclude that we must break up the concentration of wealth and power.

Why does *modus ponens* always "work" (is always valid) as a form of deductive reasoning? To answer this, recall that in chapter 6 of *Reading* we saw that an "if X, then Y" statement is called a *conditional* or *conditional statement*. To elaborate on this a bit, the "X" term is called the antecedent and the "Y" term is called the consequent. *Modus ponens* is always valid because a conditional statement tells us that the truth of the antecedent is sufficient for (is a sufficient condition of) the truth of the consequent. The second premise in this argument form tells us that the antecedent is true. That is sufficient to draw the conclusion that the consequent is true.

Modus tollens is a form of deductive argument with this simple structure:

If X, then Y.
Not Y.
Therefore, not X.

For example:
If you want to eat something for better health, eat more fiber.
You do not want to (you will not) eat more fiber.
So, you do not want to eat something for better health.

Or:
> If we're in Seattle, then it's raining.
> It's not raining.
> Therefore, we're not in Seattle.

Why does *modus tollens* always "work" (is always valid) as a form of deductive reasoning? *Modus tollens* is always valid because a conditional statement tells us that if the consequent is not true then the antecedent is not true. That is, the truth of the consequent is a necessary condition for the truth of the antecedent. The second premise in this argument form tells us that the consequent is not true. That allows us to conclude that the antecedent is not true.

Modus ponens and *modus tollens* express the lessons of necessary and sufficient conditions discussed in chapter 9 of *Reading*. That is, they both capture several related ideas. In a valid deductive argument:

- there is no way for the premise (premises) to be true and the conclusion to be false
- if the premise (premises) is true, that is sufficient for the conclusion to be true
- the truth of the conclusion is necessary for the premise (premises) to be true
- the premise (premises) may be false and the conclusion true

Each of these statements gives expression to the idea that a deductive argument just says, "there is no way for this premise to be true and the conclusion to be false," or, equivalently, "if the premise is true, then the conclusion must be true also." And, "if the conclusion is not true, then the premise cannot be true."

The two fallacies related to *modus ponens* and *modus tollens* violate these features of a valid deductive argument.

The fallacy of *denying the antecedent* has this form:

> If X, then Y.
> Not X.
> Therefore, not Y.

For example:
> If we're in Seattle, then it's raining.
> We're not in Seattle.
> Therefore, it's not raining.

Or:
> If this society has achieved social justice, then it has achieved equality of opportunity.

This society has not achieved social justice.
So, this society has not achieved equality of opportunity.

The logical error in denying the antecedent is to treat a sufficient condition as a necessary condition. This is obvious in the Seattle example; it may be more difficult to discern in the other example involving a more complex question than whether it is raining or not. In the social justice example, if equality of opportunity is only one (necessary) component of social justice, then a society may not have achieved social justice (because it is still missing the other components of that) but it still may have achieved equality of opportunity.

The fallacy of *affirming the consequent* has this form:

If X, then Y.
Y.
Therefore, X.

For example:
If we're in Seattle, then it's raining.
It's raining.
Therefore, we're in Seattle.

Or:
If this society has achieved social justice, then it has achieved equality of opportunity.
This society has achieved equality of opportunity.
So, this society has achieved social justice.

The logical error in affirming the consequent is to treat a necessary condition as a sufficient condition. This is obvious in simple examples like the Seattle example, and may be more difficult as arguments get more complex. In the social justice example, if equality of opportunity is only one (necessary) component of social justice, then achieving equality of opportunity does not imply that the society has achieved social justice.

Outside of this book and other texts discussing logic, it is extremely unlikely that you will ever see an author (or speaker) declaring, "and as proven by *modus ponens* . . ." or "as proven by *modus tollens* . . ." Yet authors commonly use these forms of deductive reasoning in argumentative texts. They also commonly commit the related fallacies of denying the antecedent and affirming the consequent. Understanding these two argument forms and the two related fallacies will enhance your understanding of argumentative texts, including understanding the limits of the power of arguments that may otherwise sound very persuasive.

With these argument forms, and the two related fallacies, in mind, work through the following exercises.

9.19. Are these arguments valid or invalid? If valid, what argument form do they employ? If invalid, which fallacy do they commit?

   a. If Winston Churchill was a great wartime leader and historian, he would have won the Nobel Prize for Literature.
      Churchill was a great wartime leader and historian.
      Therefore, Churchill won the Nobel Prize for Literature.
   b. If Churchill won the Nobel Prize for Literature, then it is because he was a great wartime leader and historian.
      Churchill was a great wartime leader and historian.
      So, Churchill did win the Nobel Prize for Literature.
   c. If Churchill was a great historian, then he won the Nobel Prize for Literature.
      Churchill won the Nobel Prize for Literature.
      Accordingly, Churchill was a great historian.
   d. If Churchill was a great historian, then he won the Nobel Prize for Literature.
      Churchill was not a great historian.
      Accordingly, Churchill did not win the Nobel Prize for Literature.
   e. To create widespread prosperity, we must break up the concentration of wealth and power.
      We will break up the concentration of wealth and power.
      Therefore, we will create widespread prosperity.
   f. If we want to create widespread prosperity, then we must break up the concentration of wealth and power.
      We will (must) not break up the concentration of wealth and power.
      Therefore, we do not want widespread prosperity.
   g. If we want to create widespread prosperity, then we must break up the concentration of wealth and power.
      We do not want widespread prosperity.
      Accordingly, it is not the case that we must break up the concentration of wealth and power.

NOTE

1. Thich Nhat Hanh, *The Heart of Buddha's Teaching*, p. 5 (New York: Harmony 2015).

Appendix A
Answer Key

This Answer Key provides answers to most of the questions asked in the exercises and case studies. If the answer to a question can be found in the text of a chapter of *Reading*, I generally have not included it here unless the point is especially worth reinforcing. For the most part, these are answers to the more difficult or more debatable questions asked in the exercises and case studies.

CHAPTER 1. INTRODUCTION

1.1.   a. False
       b. False
       c. True
       d. False
       e. False
       f. True
       g. True

1.2.   a.–e. A reasonable case could be made that this paragraph does *not* state an argument.

Consider sentences [1] and [2]. You may be tempted to think that they state a theoretical argument. But these sentences are not trying to argue for the truth of any conclusion based on the truth of any other statements. So, they do not state an argument. At best, they provide an explanation of the cause of the mass extinction of the dinosaurs millions of years ago. (An explanation of the causes of an event or state of affairs is called a *causal explanation.* See chapter 4 of *Reading.*)

Do sentences [3] through [6] state an argument? Do they argue for the truth of a conclusion based on reasoning from one or more premises? Do sentences [3] through [6] include a conclusion? Sentence [6] is the most obvious candidate, but how does that statement follow logically from sentences [3] through [5]? Maybe sentence [6] is just a statement of the author's opinion and not a conclusion that follows logically from any of the other sentences. If there is no conclusion, there is no argument. So, you reasonably could conclude that this passage does not state an argument.

Yet, if you read this passage in a letter to the editor of a newspaper or a blog, you may ask yourself, why would the author write this if he was not trying to assert an argument? Is he writing the piece just to scare us about the future? That would be silly.

A more likely reason for his writing the piece is that he is trying to make a practical argument, even if it is not clearly and completely set forth. The practical argument would be this:

> The United States government is not prepared to prevent a gigantic asteroid from hitting the earth. [Premise]
> There is a substantial risk that such an impact could occur in the next 25 years. [Premise]
> If it does, it will end all civilization as we know it, cause billions of people to die painful, miserable, excruciating deaths, and, for any humans who survive, existence will be like living in the Stone Age. [Premise]
> We all want to avoid mass suffering and civilization-ending disasters. [Implied premise]
> Accordingly, the United States government needs to (should or ought to) research how to prevent another massive asteroid collision. [Conclusion]

We are able to interpret sentences [3] through [6] as stating a practical argument by (1) implying a missing premise and (2) interpreting the phrase "needs to" in sentence [6] as equivalent to "should" or "ought to." Notice that if we did not provide the implied premise, we would have three factual premises, but they would not lead to the conclusion that our government should do anything. You can test this by supposing that no one wants to avoid mass suffering and civilization-ending disasters. If that were the case, then the conclusion would not follow from the first three premises.

Assume that the author intended to make this argument. What is the connection between that argument and the causal explanation in sentences [1] and [2]? Those first two sentences are not part of the argument, so why are they there? Presumably, the author's intent in including the causal explanation of the extinction of the dinosaurs is to add a sense of urgency or importance to his *practical* argument. He would be trying to communicate something like this—"it happened once, it can happen again; this is not just a theoretical possibility."

1.2.   f.–g. The language quoted is there for its rhetorical effect. The argument of the paragraph does not require this language; the conclusion would still follow from the premises even without this language.

CHAPTER 2. READING IS NOT A SPECTATOR SPORT

2.1. A summary is a restatement of the meaning of a text in condensed form, usually in a sentence, several sentences, or a paragraph, whichever you think is most appropriate given the length and nature of the text you are summarizing. Depending on the context in which you are asked to summarize a work, and the type of text you are being asked to summarize (an entire book, a chapter, a short article?), you may also need to identify the text by stating (1) the name of the author and (2) the title of the work you are summarizing. Chapter 6 in *Reading* expands on this definition. It is adequate for our present purposes.

CHAPTER 3. WHY ARE YOU READING?

3.1.   a. False

b. True

c. False

d. False. These are the three principal purposes of reading. You also could read just for fun (which is often why we read comics or novels) or to distract yourself (which is why dentists and doctors have magazines in their waiting areas).

3.3.   It is to attempt, as nearly as is possible, to understand what thoughts or emotions the author intends to communicate to the reader, what the author means.

3.4.   It is a very good description of reading for understanding. Compare this passage with the passage from Mark Edmundson quoted in chapter 3 of *Reading* and the surrounding discussion.

CHAPTER 4. ARGUMENTS: A CLOSER LOOK

4.1. a. False. Consider this deductive argument, in addition to the ones discussed in chapter 4 of *Reading*. Both of its premises and its conclusion are general (all, every, none, no) statements.

No students in the 5th grade class are left-handed.

No students in the 5th grade class are ambidextrous.

Every person is either right-handed, left-handed, or ambidextrous.

So, all students in the 5th grade class are right-handed.

b. False

c. False

d. True

e. False

f. False. Inductive arguments are either strong or weak. None are invalid.

g. False

h. False

i. True

j. False

k. True

l. True

m. False

n. True

o. False

p. False

q. False

r. False

s. True

t. True

u. False

v. True

w. True

4.2. Suppose that by a stroke of good luck you have been invited to a Hollywood party where many actors are present. You do not know or recognize many of them. Being a sociable person, you start talking to a person *who you do not know* about how much you like the

Appendix A

most recent *Star Wars* movies. You know that Jason Suotamo is the actor who played Chewbacca in these movies. After a few minutes, the person you are talking to says, "I'm the actor who played Chewbacca in those movies." You can formulate an argument that the person you are talking to is Jason Suotamo, like this:

> Jason Suotamo is the actor who played Chewbacca in the most recent *Star Wars* movies. [Premise]
> "I played Chewbacca in the most recent *Star Wars* movies." [Premise, as spoken by the person I am talking to.]
> Therefore, the person I am talking to is Jason Suotamo. [Conclusion, as thought by you]

If the premises are true, there is no way the conclusion can be false. (This is a straightforward deductive-theoretic argument.)

Myth #1 in effect states that you cannot draw this conclusion from these premises, just because the conclusion is a statement of an objective fact. Myth #1 says that you cannot use your power of reasoning to draw an inference as to the identity of the person you are talking to. This example, and your own experience, tells you the opposite. As soon as you hear, "I played Chewbacca in the most recent *Star Wars* movies," your deductive reasoning kicks in and you are very likely to respond, "Oh, wow, you are Jason Suotamo! I'm so glad to meet you." (The philosopher John Perry uses a similar example to make a point about the nature of knowledge in his book, *Knowledge, Possibility, Consciousness,* p. 119 [Cambridge: MIT Press 2001].)

4.3. Any practical argument will show Myth #2 to be wrong.

4.4. a. A person who practices basketball every day will be good at basketball.
   He practices basketball every day.
   So, he is good at basketball.

   b. A person who lies repeatedly is not trustworthy.
   Donald lies (has lied) repeatedly.
   Therefore, Donald is not trustworthy (I don't trust Donald.).

   c. Anyone who belongs to that family is a liar and a crook.
   Eric belongs to that family.
   So, Eric is a liar and a crook.

   d. All good Communists have studied the works of Karl Marx.
   You have not studied the works of Karl Marx.
   So, you are not a good Communist.

4.5. Here is one simple example:

How do I know he's lying? His lips are moving.

Started more formally:

Every time his lips are moving (*i.e.,* every time he talks), he lies.

His lips are moving.

Therefore, (I know) he is lying.

4.7. a.–c. Berry is not trying to prove that "a healthy ecosystem requires heavily forested areas," or that "this natural beauty should be preserved for its own sake," or anything else. Berry has painted a word picture in this paragraph, *describing* where he lives and the surrounding land. This is a descriptive paragraph, that is all.

4.8. The subject of the essay is about the tone of the political debate in the United States over global warming. It is not about the reality of global warming or solutions to it. Easterbrook believes that this debate is marked by "gloom" and a lack of "environmental optimism." You could reasonably read this as either an argumentative text or as an explanatory text, or both. At the end of the second paragraph Easterbrook asks the question, "Why is such environmental optimism absent from American political debate?" The remainder of the article could be read as offering a causal explanation of this lack of optimism or as an argument for one answer to this question. If you read the text as offering an argument, does the last sentence of the text answer the question asked or does it provide an answer to a different question, namely, why we have not yet solved the problem of global warming?

4.9. a. The essay states two interrelated arguments. Here is a reasonable restatement of them.

Allocation of scarce medical resources should be made to realize the best medical (health) outcomes for the most people.

Covid-19 is causing beds and ventilators in intensive care units ("ICUs") to become scarce.

Therefore, beds and ventilators in ICUs should be allocated to realize the best medical (health) outcomes for the most people. [First conclusion]

The "best medical outcomes" means those outcomes defined by objective measures of medical benefit to patients.

These objective measures include (a) assessing which patients will get little medical benefit from the use of scarce resources because they have a medical condition such as cancer, liver or heart failure, or the like where death is imminent even if they receive the

Appendix A 77

scarce resources and (b) assessing which patients are more likely to get real medical benefit from the use of scarce resources and recover from Covid-19.

Criteria such as ethnicity, gender, ability to pay, family pressure, or who got to the hospital first are irrelevant to defining what counts as the "best medical outcomes" for patients and should not be used to allocate scarce medical resources.

Accordingly, to realize the best medical (health) outcomes for the most people, scarce medical resources (ICU beds and ventilators) should be denied to or withdrawn from patients for whom the chances of the best medical outcomes are minimal or nonexistent and provided to patients for whom the best medical outcomes are likely to be real and lead to recovery. [Second conclusion]

Significantly, the conclusion of the first argument also acts as a premise for the second argument.

b. Both of the arguments are deductive. The authors are not stating that their conclusions follow only with more or less likelihood or probability, as they would if the arguments were inductive. They are articulating certain moral rules and a definition of "best medical outcomes" and applying these to what they take to be a factual situation (the scarcity of medical resources caused by Covid-19) to reach conclusions which necessarily follow. (The conclusion of the second argument is action-guiding, so that argument is a deductive-practical argument.)

4.10. a. Contrary to the perceptions created by the Trump administration and held by some Americans, refugees are not a burden to or a drain on the American economy, but actually contribute to (energize) it.

b. Inductive.

c. As written, the argument appears to be strong, because of the many studies cited by the author. More research would need to be done on the studies relied upon and other available studies to determine whether the argument is strong or weak in light of all available data and possible methods of analysis of that data.

4.11. a. Reading is like watching football (because both are passive activities that require few distractions).

b. It is an inductive argument by analogy. An argument by analogy generally has this form:

X (which is a thing or activity) has properties A, B, and C.

Y (some other thing or activity) also has properties A and B.

Therefore, Y probably has property C.

c. Weak. Because reading and watching football are said to have two properties in common (being passive and requiring few distractions) does not mean that reading shares any other property with watching football or is like watching football in any other respect. For example, reading an argumentative text for understanding attempts to discern the meaning the author intends to communicate, which often requires active analysis. Watching a football game does not involve attempting to discern anyone's meaning and does not necessarily involve any active analysis.

Case Study: The *Gettysburg Address*

4.12.   a. This is a reasonable restatement of the argument of the text. More detailed restatements are possible, especially depending on how one interprets the sentences relating to the dedication of the cemetery.

Our civil war is a test of whether our nation, or any nation, founded on the ideals of liberty and equality, can endure (as a united nation) for a long time.

The soldiers who died here at Gettysburg gave their lives so that our nation (founded on these ideals) might endure ("live").

These soldiers cannot carry on their work for this cause. [Implied premise]

But, we can and ought to dedicate ourselves here and now ("It is rather for us to be here dedicated"; "that we here highly resolve") to the cause ("the unfinished work") which the soldiers died for and have advanced.

That cause is the rebirth ("new birth") of freedom in a united nation ("this nation, under God").

Our dedication to that cause will ensure the endurance of government of the people, by the people, for the people.

A government of the people, by the people, for the people is a government ("nation") of liberty and equality.

Accordingly, we ought ("it is rather for us") to dedicate ourselves today to the same cause the soldiers died for to ensure that our united nation, founded on the ideals of liberty and equality, will long endure.

b. It is an inductive-practical argument. Based on selected historical facts and facts about the ongoing Civil War, Lincoln is urging his listeners, and in turn all of the citizens of the North, to dedicate themselves to the work of rebuilding a nation dedicated to the ideals of liberty and equality, *i.e.,* to do something to ensure the survival of free government.

c. 1."Four score and seven years ago our fathers brought forth on this continent, a new nation, conceived in Liberty, and dedicated to the proposition that all men are created equal."

Literally, the sentence means, "This nation was founded eighty-seven years ago on the ideals of liberty and equality."

2. "We are met on a great battle-field of that war. We have come to dedicate a portion of that field, as a final resting place for those who here gave their lives that that nation might live. It is altogether fitting and proper that we should do this."

Literally, "We are gathered here at the cemetery on the Gettysburg battlefield to honor the soldiers who died to preserve our nation. It is appropriate that we do this."

3. "But, in a larger sense, we can not dedicate—we can not consecrate—we can not hallow—this ground. The brave men, living and dead, who struggled here, have consecrated it, far above our poor power to add or detract. The world will little note, nor long remember what we say here, but it can never forget what they did here."

Literally, "The brave men who fought at Gettysburg have consecrated this ground through their actions and our words are inadequate to consecrate it any more than that. Our words will be forgotten, but their deeds will not be."

d. The text is almost entirely argumentative and rhetorical. Certain sentences may be read as descriptive. For example, "Now we are engaged in a great civil war, testing whether that nation, or any nation so conceived and so dedicated, can long endure. We are met on a great battle-field of that war. We have come to dedicate a portion of that field, as a final resting place for those who here gave their lives that that nation might live." Yet these sentences are so ladened with argumentative points and rhetorical phrases that it is difficult to read them as primarily descriptive. The first of these sentences, for example, rather than describing anything, is better read as stating the political problem facing the United States and all countries founded on the ideals of liberty and democracy, namely, whether the pervasiveness of liberty and equality causes the dissolution of the functioning political order.

CHAPTER 5. EVERY PERSON HAS A SKELETON, EVERY ARGUMENT HAS A STRUCTURE

Exercises

5.1. Asking a question, stating a problem.

This may be a bit hard to see, since the first sentence of the speech states a fact, in very rhetorical terms: "Four score and seven years ago our fathers brought forth on this continent, a new nation, conceived in Liberty, and dedicated to the proposition that all men are created equal." The second sentence of the speech, however, views the Civil War as an attempt to answer a question. In full, the sentence reads: "Now we are engaged in a great civil war, testing whether that nation, or any nation so conceived and so dedicated, can long endure." The question embedded in that sentence is: "can that nation, or any nation so conceived and so dedicated, long endure?" In modern, less rhetorical language: can a form of government that embodies widespread freedom and equality last for a long time, or will that very freedom and equality cause it to self-destruct?

5.2. The author tells us what the book is about: "the modern state—how it came into being, how it has developed, and in what directions we can expect it to change." And, he tells us that the history of warfare and the legal order (the law) of a state are parts of that broader subject. This is a good example of the Subject Variation, even though the author never uses the term "subject" and never states, for example, "the subject of this book is . . ."

5.3. Russell is introducing this chapter by asking a question or stating a problem. More accurately, he is asking two questions, namely, (1) what is the value of philosophy and (2) why should it be studied.

5.4. This introduction offers a clear statement of the author's thesis, namely, that there are three types of violence, which he terms "subjective," "symbolic," and "systemic." It then sets forth a general statement of the elements of the premises by which he is going to prove his thesis. And it concludes with a statement of the implications of, or lessons to be drawn from, his thesis and proof. That is a good example of the Road Map introduction.

5.5. If you read just the first paragraph to be the introduction, it is an anecdotal introduction. If the first three paragraphs are the introduction, then it is a form of asking a question (stating a problem) introduction. It asks, at the end of the third paragraph, "what exactly is it . . .we all get" from the system of elite education that is in place in this country?"

5.6. You could read it as either a Subject Variation or anecdotal introduction. The paragraph at the end of the introduction begins, "These questions are what this book is all about." In other words, these types of questions are the subject of this book. Because the introduction begins with a hypothetical example in the nature of an anecdote ("Imagine that you are sitting . . ."), you may also reasonably read this as stating an anecdotal introduction. Note, however, that because this ice cream example is hypothetical, it differs from the fact-based anecdotal introductions we considered in chapter 5 of *Reading*.

5.7. a.–b. The first paragraph is the introduction. It can be read as stating a problem and responding to it. As stated by Dr. King, the problem is whether his illegal, nonviolent activities in Birmingham are "'unwise and untimely'" as charged in the "recent statement" by the eight clergymen. Or, the problem can be stated as a question: "Are my (Dr. King's) activities of civil disobedience in Birmingham unwise and untimely?" The rest of this essay is his answer to this question.

c. Dr. King does not expressly state a thesis in this Letter. This is highly unusual in an argumentative text.

d. The essay can be read either as a point-by-point rebuttal of each of the particular charges leveled by the clergymen or as trying to prove one broad, unstated point. For example, paragraphs 2, 3, and 4 are an argument against the claim that "outsiders" like Dr. King should not come into a city like Birmingham to protest. Dr. King's argument in response to this charge can be stated as follows:

> I was invited to come to Birmingham by residents of this city to conduct a nonviolent direct action program. These residents are affiliated with the Southern Christian Leadership Conference, of which I am the President. [Paragraph 2]
> I am morally compelled to carry the gospel of freedom beyond my home town, just as did the prophets of the Old Testament and St. Paul in the New Testament. [Paragraph 3]
> Injustice anywhere is a threat to justice everywhere. [Paragraph 4]
> (We know this because:)
> All communities and states are interrelated; whatever affects one person directly in one community or state affects all persons indirectly wherever they live. [Paragraph 4]
> The political union of the United States [or the American idea of freedom] means that anyone who is a citizen of the United States cannot be considered an outsider at any place within the United States. [Paragraph 4]

Accordingly, legally and morally, I am no more an "outsider" who does not belong in Birmingham than is anyone who calls Birmingham home.

Similar arguments could be reconstructed for the other sections of the Letter.

e. Dr. King's *implicit* thesis is: "I was morally justified in performing and leading illegal nonviolent acts of civil disobedience in Birmingham at that time in order to secure the equality, liberties, and human rights of African-Americans." This implicit thesis is his solution to the problem expressed in the introduction, namely, whether his activities of illegal civil disobedience are "unwise and untimely."

With this statement of Dr. King's thesis, reconstruct the argument of the essay.

5.9. This is not an example of one of the six kinds of introductions we examined in chapter 5 of *Reading*. As noted in that chapter, those six are not exhaustive of all of the possible types of introductions. Some argumentative texts introduce a term, define it, and then make an argument based on or related to that definition. That is what this introduction does. It gives you a definition of "patriotism" and then tells you that the rest of the text will elaborate on this meaning through examples. We can call this a "Definitional" introduction.

Case Study: An Op-Ed on the Meaning of the 4th of July

5.10. a. The only statements that may support this statement are the first sentence of the first paragraph and, possibly, the first sentence of the last paragraph. If the text is intended to state an argument for the truth of the second sentence of the first paragraph, it is a very weak inductive argument. That argument would be:

> The Fourth of July has become another national holiday whose great historical significance will be overshadowed by sales at the mall, barbecues, and other social events. [Premise]
> This day [July 4th] is not about hot dogs, beer, shopping and fireworks. [Premise]
> The real meaning of the 4th of July is gradually being forgotten. [Conclusion]

If the author were trying to prove that the "real meaning" of July 4th is gradually being forgotten, offering two statements of opinion as to how Americans celebrate the day is hardly adequate. One would expect, for example, that he would rely on public opinion surveys that track over several years Americans' views on the meaning of the holiday, evidence on the number of patriotic parades held each year on this day, evidence on the number of ceremonies honoring soldiers who died in battle, evidence on the number of people who participate in such patriotic events, and a comparison of this data to the number of people who go shopping or attend barbeques or other non-patriotic social events on this day.

Note that the statements in the middle paragraphs of this piece—all of which refer to events in the past—may support the author's views on the "real meaning" of July 4th, but they are not relevant to his opinion as to whether that "real meaning" is being gradually forgotten in the present.

b. Most of the statements in the third, fourth, and fifth paragraphs are offered as support for this statement of the "true meaning" of July 4th. Also, this statement from paragraph 2 may be read as support for the statement of the "true meaning": "These men were aware of the dangers and challenges that lay ahead by taking such a bold step." This statement in effect says, "these men sacrificed their own interests intentionally and knowingly, not by accident or happenstance."

c. The inductive argument that sacrifice is the "true meaning" of July 4th is weak. In one fashion or another, similar arguments could be made about the personal sacrifices that were made to establish ancient Rome, or modern France during and after the French Revolution, or many other nations. Moreover, the sacrifice that the author praises was for the sake of noble ideals—unalienable rights, liberty, and equality—and not just for the sake of founding a nation on other ideals or on no ideals at all. One might reasonably think that any statement of the "true meaning" of July 4th would include the power of such ideals to move people to do great actions.

d. Either the title of the essay or the last sentence of the first paragraph can make a reasonable claim to being the thesis of the argument. Note that the author has presented much more, and more compelling, evidence in support of the statement about the "real meaning" of July 4th than he offers for the statement that we are gradually forgetting the meaning of July 4th. That is one indication that he intends the title to state the thesis.

Or, the thesis may be a combination of these two statements, as in, for example, "We (Americans) are gradually forgetting that the true meaning of July 4th is sacrifice."

5.11. Considered as a piece of rhetoric, the piece fares well. The opinions and sentiments expressed in this text are patriotic and noble. The author marshals facts about the sacrifices made by the founding fathers and their families that, presumably, are not known to most Americans and that show the depth and extent of the commitments made by these early Americans to this nascent nation. Moreover, the author's contrasts of these sacrifices and acts of courage to our current trivial "celebrations" of the 4th of July—barbeques, trips to the mall, and fireworks—compel the reader to reflect on what it is that we really should be celebrating on July 4th.

From an argumentative perspective, there is much to be desired in this piece. It is not clear whether the author's thesis is to be found in the title, the last sentence of the first paragraph, or in some combination of these. Rather than stating and clarifying the thesis, the introduction obscures it. Moreover, the inductive arguments in support of the title statement and the last sentence of the first paragraph are weak.

Accordingly, it appears that the author intends this text to be principally rhetorical and not argumentative, although it clearly is partially argumentative.

CHAPTER 6. WHAT DOES THE SKELETON LOOK LIKE? OUTLINES AND SUMMARIES

Exercises

6.1. The article, "Study Latin if you want to talk like a supervillain," by Frankie Thomas, initially appeared on the PBS NewsHour in April 2018. In the article, Ms. Thomas highlights one benefit of studying Latin—"talking like a supervillain"—as a way of grabbing the reader's attention. She also discusses other benefits of studying Latin: it has all of the pleasures of a puzzle, time capsule, and a secret code; it is like ghost-hunting; it immerses the learner in the world of war, gods, gladiators, and murderous barbers; Latin is a beautiful language; and because it is a "dead" language, it teaches the important lesson that nothing is permanent, not even the learner or the author. In sum, the reader is urged to study Latin because it will change the learner's life for the better in numerous ways.

6.3. b.–c. The thesis is at the end of the second paragraph. It can be restated as: "The Trump Administration's decision on Feb. 1, 2019, to withdraw the U.S. from the Intermediate-Range Nuclear Forces treaty is a decision that makes the world a more competitive, combustible place in the long term, not immediately."

The premises for the conclusion are the three points identified in this summary of the text.

"The end of a U.S.-Russia arms treaty spells long-term trouble," is an opinion piece written by Ian Bremmer; it appeared in *Time* in February 2019. In this essay, Mr. Bremmer argues that the decision by the Trump Administration in February 2019 to withdraw from the Intermediate-Range Nuclear Forces ("INF") treaty will make the world a riskier, less safe place in the long-run. He argues for this conclusion by stating that the U.S.'s withdrawal: (1) will weaken U.S.-European relations, (2) may cause China to increase its military build-up in response to possible increased Russian and U.S. missile deployments in Asia, which were forbidden under the treaty, and (3) will contribute to the deterioration of U.S.-Russian relations, which are already bad as a result of many other points of tension and which may lead to conflict. He concludes that the INF treaty and arms control generally were points of possible collaboration between the U.S. and Russia, but now they are one more point of tension between them.

6.4. b. This is a reasonable summary of the essay:

"Letter from a Birmingham Jail" was written by Dr. Martin Luther King, Jr. in April 1963. The essay takes the form of an extended rebuttal to a statement published by eight white clergymen criticizing Dr. King for coming to Birmingham, Alabama (from Atlanta, Georgia) to lead and participate in illegal, but nonviolent, civil rights protests. Dr. King addresses each of the major points made by the clergymen and argues that he was morally justified in performing and leading illegal nonviolent acts of civil disobedience in Birmingham at that time in order to secure the equality, liberty, and human rights of African-Americans.

6.5. c. The essay could reasonably be read as being an expository essay. The author is in effect stating, "I'm going *to show you* (present or expose to you) the several disadvantages of an elite education." If you read the text in this fashion, then you will find arguments embedded within the exposition.

d. Inductive-theoretical.

6.7. "Antidotes for fear" is a sermon written by Dr. Martin Luther King, Jr. In the sermon, Dr. King argues that we cannot eliminate fear in our lives, but we can master it by employing four techniques. These techniques are: (1) unflinchingly knowing our fears and honestly asking ourselves why we are afraid; (2) exercising the virtue of courage; (3) love; and (4) having faith. In support of his contention that these are the four ways to master fear, Dr. King presents various anecdotes, quotations, analysis of concepts, analysis of then-current social and international relations, and a reflection on Christian faith. Of these four techniques, Dr. King appears to believe (he is not entirely clear on this) that faith is the most effective way of mastering fear, and specifically, the faith that "God's gonna take care of you."

6.9. Here is a reasonable outline of Section I.

1. The first method to master fear is to unflinchingly face our fears and honestly ask ourselves why we are afraid (*i.e.*, to confront our fears).
2. This confrontation gives us some power to master our fears because through it we learn that:
    a. some fears are residues of childhood need or apprehension
    b. some fears are outgrowths of our relations with our parents
    c. some fears are more imaginary than real, and
    d. some fears involve the misuse of imagination.

Do not be concerned if your outline and mine differ in some respects. Instead, ask yourself whether your outline captures more than the essential points Dr. King is making in this Section and whether it omits any essential points.

6.10. Dr. King's argument in Section I can be restated as:

1. By unflinchingly facing our fears and honestly asking ourselves why we are afraid we learn that:
   a. some fears are residues of childhood need or apprehension
   b. some fears are outgrowths of our relations with our parents
   c. some fears are more imaginary than real, and
   d. some fears involve the misuse of imagination.
2. This knowledge of our fears and their origins gives us power to master our fears.
3. Therefore, unflinchingly facing our fears and honestly asking ourselves why we are afraid is one way to master our fears.

Once we reformulate our outline into Dr. King's argument in Section I, we see that Dr. King is arguing that to know our fears and their origins is to have power over our fears. Or, in Section I, Dr. King is arguing that having knowledge (of our fears and their origins) is to have control over ourselves.

To distill the argument even further: knowledge is power. That is at once a strong, bold statement and a bit puzzling. Why is knowledge something other than what you have once you have gathered a bunch of facts or data rather than a recognition of our emotional states? And why is power having knowledge, rather than having charisma, or being a leader, or having physical strength? You can ponder these questions at your leisure.

For now, it is sufficient that you understand that Dr. King's sermon is touching new ground for most of us, that he is making a point that he believes is profound and, if it were really understood and acted upon by each of us, could change each of our lives. This is just one example of how reading for understanding enriches your life and empowers you.

6.11. Here is my outline of Section II of "Antidotes for fear."

1. We can master fear through one of the supreme virtues, namely, courage.
   a. Plato's, Aristotle's, and St. Thomas Aquinas' views on courage are mentioned.
2. Courage is defined as "the power of the mind to overcome fear."
   a. Fear has a definite object, which may be faced, attacked, analyzed, and endured.
3. Courage takes the fear produced by an object into itself and thereby conquers the fear.

4. Courage is defined a second time, as self-affirmation in spite of what tends to hinder the self from affirming itself (quoting Paul Tillich).
   a. This definition is refined as, "self-affirmation in spite of death and nonbeing . . . ."
5. Courageous self-affirmation is not selfishness; it includes a proper self-love and love of others.
6. Courage (defined a third time as "the determination not to be overwhelmed by any object, however frightful . . .") enables us to stand up to any fear.
   a. These feared objects are not imaginary (are not "snakes under the carpet"), but rather are part of human experience.
   b. These objects ("forces") threaten to negate life and must be challenged by courage (which once again is defined, this time as "the power of life to affirm itself in spite of life's ambiguities").
7. Courage and cowardice are antithetical.
   a. Courage is defined, once again, as "an inner resolution to go forward in spite of obstacles and frightening situations"; cowardice is submissive self-surrender to circumstances.
      i. Courage and cowardice are contrasted in three additional, similar ways.
8. The Section concludes with the admonition, "We must constantly build dikes of courage to hold back the flood of fear."

6.12. Does your statement of Dr. King's thesis look like this?

> Dr. King's thesis is that fear cannot be eliminated, but may be mastered by four techniques, namely, (1) facing our fears honestly and asking ourselves why we are afraid, (2) having courage, (3) through love, and (4) through faith in God. Dr. King's thesis may also include the proposition that of these four, faith in God is the most important, but his sermon is not entirely clear about that.

In other words, Dr. King's thesis is that we cannot eliminate fear and can only master it; there are four ways of mastering fear, and they are 1, 2, 3, and 4.

Note that even though there are two main arguments in Dr. King's sermon (one in the introduction and one in sections I through IV), this statement of his thesis combines the conclusions of those two arguments. It states the conclusion of the introduction (fear cannot be eliminated) and of the next four sections (it can only be mastered, and there are four ways to do that). Although Dr. King has two main arguments, he has joined them into one sermon, presumably to make one broad point to his congregation. That is why your statement of his thesis better reflects Dr. King's intent when it includes the conclusions of both arguments, and does not treat the sermon as having two separate theses.

6.13. The introduction states an inductive-theoretical argument. The conclusion of the argument does not express any uncertainty, probability, or mere likelihood, which are common characteristics of inductive arguments. Nonetheless, the argument is employing a series of factual statements to draw a conclusion. A different set of facts or additional facts may require the conclusion to be abandoned or modified. That is a principal characteristic of inductive arguments. Dr. King's conclusion would be better stated, from a purely logical point of view, to acknowledge that it is only probable, even if he believes it is highly probable. That, of course, would cause the argument to lose a certain measure of its rhetorical force. The remainder of the sermon states an inductive-practical argument.

CHAPTER 7. AMBIGUITY AND NONLITERAL USES OF LANGUAGE

Exercises

7.1. a. The sentence is ambiguous. It expresses both an idea of moral interconnectedness and an idea of causal (physical) interconnectedness. The phrase "inescapable network of mutuality" seems intended to capture the idea of moral obligations that we mutually owe to each other, the idea that "yes, you are your brother's keeper" (recall Cain's question in the Old Testament). This meaning is reinforced by the use of the moral concept of justice in the prior sentence ("Injustice anywhere is a threat to justice everywhere."). The phrase "tied in a single garment of destiny" suggests that an injustice that happens to one person will have effects felt by everyone else, that our communal life has close bonds of cause and effect. This causal meaning is reinforced by the sentence immediately following ("Whatever affects one directly, affects all indirectly.").

c. One way to test whether a statement is intended to be rhetorical is to ask whether or not it is literally true. Is the sentence under consideration—"Injustice anywhere is a threat to justice everywhere"—literally true? Suppose a child is bullied one time in an elementary school in California. Is that injustice a threat to justice in Amsterdam? In Singapore? Of course, every false statement is not literally true, and yet many of them are not rhetorical. So, this test must be applied with care.

7.2. a.–b. "Elite education" is ambiguous. In paragraph 3, the author states that "elite education" refers to "the whole system in which these [cultural and political] skirmishes play out. *Not just the Ivy League and its peer institutions*, but also the mechanisms that get you there in the first place; the private and affluent public 'feeder' schools, the ever-growing parastructure of tutors and test-prep courses and enrichment programs, the whole admissions frenzy and everything that leads up to and away from it." (Italics added.) In other parts of the essay, *e.g.*, paragraphs 4 and 5, he uses "elite education" more narrowly to refer to "elite schools," and specifically Ivy League schools.

c. This example will get you started. In paragraph 12 the author employs an example of a friend who was a waitress and who received a D in a class at Cleveland State University. The example intended to be rhetorical, in large part. We can assume that the author recognizes that one example is insufficient to *prove* his point. (It would be a single premise in a weak inductive argument.) So, the author has not employed the example for that logical purpose. Moreover, he concedes in the following paragraph that this example may be "extreme." So, it has even less weight as a premise in an inductive argument.

But the use of an "extreme" example here is not necessarily a rhetorical weakness. To the contrary. Because it is "extreme," it more powerfully grips the emotions or our sense of fairness—she was working as a waitress while going to college (she's a hard worker with initiative), had an A in this course (she's smart enough to succeed in this course), but then she received a D *just* because she turned in her paper an hour late. Your sense of justice shouts, "That's really unfair," especially when contrasted with the many "second chances" students get at elite schools like Yale.

In light of this, consider whether the first paragraph of the essay is intended to be rhetorical. If so, how does it appeal to our emotions or feelings?

7.3. It is a prudential normative statement. The author is saying that if the goal is to reduce greenhouse-gas emissions (to address climate change) in the most effective manner, then the proper policy response, from an agricultural perspective, is to improve agricultural practices. So, the "should" in this sentence reflects a prudential norm of taking the most effective means of accomplishing an end. That is, whatever the purpose of our action, we should (for prudential reasons) want to accomplish it efficiently.

7.4. a. These are two of the more clearly normative statements in this essay:

"But it is not just ethically acceptable to prioritize treatment for a patient more likely to benefit compared with another, it is an ethical imperative." (Paragraph 7)

"Medical care is a shared societal resource to be applied where it is most effective." (Paragraph 8)

b. The last sentence of the essay is a normative statement. It implicitly states the moral principle that, when the rationing of medical equipment and treatments is necessary, that rationing is morally permitted or morally required if it achieves the best outcomes for the most people. (That is a version of the moral principle called Utilitarianism, which says that actions are moral if they promote the greatest good for the greatest number of people. We briefly encountered Utilitarianism in chapter 8 of *Reading*.)

7.5. Here are two normative statements in the essay, to get you started. (1) Paragraph 1, the second sentence, which states that Cleveland's character was "solid" and "admirable" and that it had these qualities in degrees not seen since Washington. (2) Paragraph 2, first sentence, ascribing to Cleveland the trait of "steadfastness," and to a high degree, *i.e.*, "vast."

7.6. If you interpret this editorial as principally a rhetorical, and not an argumentative, text, then at least the first and last paragraphs are rhetorical, since they are designed to contrast the noble acts of our founders with the trivial acts by which we celebrate July 4th.

7.7. The President apparently intended to make three points in this sentence, namely, that his inauguration (1) celebrates how a free people transfer power and is not just the result of a partisan victory in the last presidential election, (2) is both an end of something and the beginning of something else, and (3) points to both renewal and change. Imagine you were in the audience listening to this speech. Compare the emotional impact of President Kennedy's opening rhetorical statement with my comparatively bland three-part, literal restatement of it.

Case Study: "All Men Are Created Equal"

7.13. a. It is hard to see how it does state an argument on this subject. It states two "self-evident" truths, as follows:

All people ("all men") have unalienable rights.

The purpose of a (just) government ("governments are instituted") is to protect ("secure") these rights.

But there is no suggestion that the author intended either of these "truths" to follow from the other one by any sort of logical reasoning. The *Declaration* simply states that these are two "self-evident" truths, among others.

b. Yes. It can be stated like this:

All people ("all men") have unalienable rights. [Premise]

The purpose of a government ("governments are instituted") is to secure (or protect) these rights. [Premise]

When a government does not secure these rights ("becomes destructive of these ends"), it is the right of the citizens to abolish it and to form a new government ("to institute new government"). [Premise]

The government of Great Britain has not secured the rights of the people of the colonies in America. [Premise]

Therefore, the people of the colonies in America have the right to withdraw from the government of Britain and to form a new government. [Conclusion]

7.15. a. You might reasonably be uncertain about whether it is an argument. The word "So" in the last sentence looks like it is introducing a conclusion drawn from the prior sentences. The author apparently intends to be making an argument.

b. The argument could be formulated in two ways:

Whatever one's beliefs regarding religion, we are all seeking something better in life.

The "something better in life" that we all seek is called "happiness." [Implied premise]

So, the very motion of our life is towards happiness.

Or,

Whatever one's beliefs regarding religion, we are all seeking something better in life.

The "something better in life" that we all seek is called "happiness." [Implied premise]

So, the very purpose of our life is to seek happiness.

Note that the first formulation takes the last sentence of this passage to be the conclusion, whereas the second formulation takes the first sentence to be the conclusion. Presumably, His Holiness intends "the very motion of our life" to mean the same thing as "the very purpose of our life." And if so, he would say that these two arguments really mean the same thing. But do they? The phrase "the very motion of our life" suggests a natural impulse, almost a biological urge or physical thrust. The "very purpose," however, suggests a more or less conscious goal, the end result of all of the deliberate choices we make. Finding that sort of ambiguity in nonacademic arguments is common.

CHAPTER 8. CONTEXT IMPARTS MEANING

Exercises

8.1. The cultural contexts include the historical self-sacrificing actions of the founders and their families and the way in which Americans conduct themselves in recent times on the 4th of July (barbeques, shopping trips, etc.).

8.2. Several passages in the speech are designed to add meaning through context. (1) "Four score and seven years ago our fathers brought forth on this continent, a new nation, conceived in Liberty, and dedicated to the proposition that all men are created equal." Lincoln is placing his speech in the intellectual and political context of the history of the founding of this nation and the ideals embodied in its founding documents, especially the *Declaration of Independence*. (2) "Now we are engaged in a great civil war, testing whether that nation, or any nation so conceived and so dedicated, can long endure." Lincoln moves from the past to the present social and cultural context of the war to pose the problem that the Civil War will answer (union or dis-union). (3) "We are met on a great battlefield of that war. We have come to dedicate a portion of that field, as a final resting place for those who here gave their lives that that nation might live. It is altogether fitting and proper that we should do this." Lincoln uses physical environment (geographical context), the battlefield and the cemetery, to focus his audience on the sacrifices of the soldiers who fought at Gettysburg and to set up the contrast, drawn a few sentences later, between those deeds and his own words. Notice specifically how Lincoln subtly moves from the broad geographical context of the entire war, to the narrower space of the Gettysburg battlefield, and finally to the even smaller space of a portion of the battlefield. This narrowing of the physical environment of his speech focuses his listeners on the present time and place and on their role in answering the question of union or dis-union.

8.3. a.–d. This sentence is not essential to the author's argument, as the restatement of that argument illustrates.

The author may have intended this paragraph (i) to be rhetorical, (ii) to provide a political or social context for the essay, or (iii) to be both rhetorical and to provide context. Or, (iv) the paragraph may just not be important to understanding the essay. You would be more inclined to include or omit this paragraph from your outline depending on what you think the author intended.

It is worth emphasising that this one-sentence paragraph can be both rhetorical and provide context. Providing that context can be a way for the author to make a rhetorical appeal for the urgency of addressing this issue—"hey, this is very timely; another election is right ahead of us; we need to ("this imperative") deal with it now . . ."

8.4. a. The early 1960s, when Dr. King wrote this Letter, were a time of social and political turmoil in the United States, especially around the issue of civil rights for African-Americans. Many southern states and politicians were resisting or opposed to racial integration and the full legal and political equality of African-Americans. A substantial percentage of white Americans agreed with the goal of full equality but questioned Dr. King's methods of illegal, nonviolent protests or the timing of his use of that strategy. The statement of the eight white clergymen and Dr. King's Letter reflect this context.

Case Study: An Opinion Piece on Federal Marijuana Regulation

8.5. a. The author states his thesis in three ways.

The title of the article is one version of his thesis: "It's Time to End Any Level of Federal Marijuana Prohibition."

The last two sentences of the first paragraph also can be read as stating the author's thesis. To paraphrase these, the thesis they state is: Removing marijuana from the federal Controlled Substances Act entirely is the only sensible path forward for marijuana reform. Like alcohol, the federal government should have very little involvement in regulating marijuana.

Finally, the last sentence of the text may also state the author's thesis. It is almost identical to the title of the article: "It's time to take the sensible step and get the federal government out of marijuana prohibition altogether."

The first and third versions of the thesis state that the federal government should have no role in regulating marijuana. The second version states a less categorical view that the federal government should have "very little" involvement. This sort of inconsistency in argumentative articles in the mass media is not uncommon.

In this article, the inconsistency seems to be a minor point. Read charitably, the author seems to be saying something like, "the federal regulation of alcohol is so minimal that it does not affect people very much, and so it is as if it did not exist at all. The federal government should regulate marijuana no more than that very minimal extent, which as a practical matter is for the federal government to not regulate it at all."

b. It is an inductive-practical argument. It is an inductive argument because the author argues from certain similarities and dissimilarities between marijuana and other drugs to reason to his thesis. Paragraphs 8 and 9 make other types of claims, asserting different types of evidence to support the author's thesis. It is a practical argument because it is saying that an entity, the federal government, should stop regulating marijuana, or regulate it very lightly.

8.6. The remainder of your outline should look like this:

2. Paragraphs 2 and 3: These paragraphs state an argument based on the dissimilarities of marijuana and other Schedule I drugs. In these paragraphs, the argument is that marijuana is different from other Schedule I drugs in that it is a whole plant consisting of both therapeutic and psychoactive compounds, unlike most of the other Schedule I substances, which are discrete, identifiable compounds with no therapeutic properties. So, marijuana should not be a Schedule I drug.
3. Paragraphs 4 through the first part of paragraph 7 ("marijuana ha[s] at least as much variance in product type and potency as alcohol"): These passages argue against federal regulation based on the analogy (similarities) between alcohol and marijuana. The argument is that marijuana is like alcohol in having wide variety and potencies and so should not be regulated by the federal government any more than alcohol is, and should be regulated by the states, just as alcohol is.
4. Beginning of paragraph 7: The author offers a second argument based on dissimilarities. He argues that the "many more therapeutic and medicinal uses" of marijuana, which are not found in alcohol, make it even a better subject of state regulation than alcohol.
5. Last few sentences of paragraph 7: The author implicitly acknowledges that his arguments so far at best may only establish that marijuana should not be a Schedule I drug.
6. Paragraphs 8–10: The author offers additional facts, wholly unrelated to the similarities or dissimilarities of marijuana to other drugs, to support the conclusion that *re*scheduling marijuana to a lower Schedule in the CSA would not be a satisfactory reform of federal marijuana law.

8.7. To assess whether the author's analogy between alcohol and marijuana is a strong or weak inductive argument, it would be useful to know the answers to these sorts of questions:

- In scientific and/or legal usage, does "alcohol" refer to a "discrete, scientifically identifiable compound" like many drugs on Schedule I (paragraph 3), or does the term only have a colloquial use that refers to a wide range of consumer products (see paragraph 5)? If the former, then the similarity between alcohol and marijuana (a plant) is not as close as the author suggests.
- As the author uses the term "alcohol," it refers to a wide range of consumer products (paragraph 5), but he states that marijuana is a plant that is able to be refined or altered into a wide range of consumer products (paragraph 3). So, it would appear that he is comparing consumer products to a raw material (the plant) that can be made into consumer products. It would appear that the more accurate comparison would be between (a) the compounds in marijuana that are psychoactive and therapeutic, on the one hand, and (b) the compound (or element) in the alcoholic products he references that make those products intoxicating, on the other hand. If that refinement is made to his argument, is his argument for de-scheduling marijuana strengthened or weakened?
- In what particular respects does marijuana have "variance in product type and potency" (paragraph 7) and are there scientific studies that compare those variances with the variances in product type and potency found in alcoholic products? If the variances significantly differ, in what respects and are those differences relevant to the issue of the appropriate type of regulation of marijuana?
- Even if scientific studies find that marijuana and alcohol have comparable variance in product type and potency, is the potential for abuse of marijuana greater than, less than, or the same as that of alcohol?
- Are the short- and long-term medical effects of marijuana in any respect worse than the short- and long-term medical effect of consuming alcohol?

8.8. If the author is right about the dissimilarities between the other Schedule I drugs and marijuana, that may only establish that therapeutic CBD or CBN (derived from the marijuana plant) should not be on Schedule I; it does not establish that psychoactive THC should be removed from Schedule I. In other words, it only supports an argument for refining Schedule I to not include the therapeutic compounds, not for removing all marijuana-derived compounds altogether from Schedule I.

Note that the author also argues on the basis of a dissimilarity between marijuana and alcohol: marijuana has "many more therapeutic and medicinal uses" than alcohol (paragraph 7). He cites no studies or facts to support this statement. He ignores, for example, that alcohol (or alcohol-based products) is commonly used in medical settings to disinfect areas of the skin before injections or incisions are made and that alcohol is commonly found in hand sanitizers.

8.9. Paragraph 8 essentially argues that rescheduling marijuana is not a viable solution to federal regulation of marijuana because it does not solve (a) certain problems that have arisen in those states that have legalized marijuana and (b) problems imposed by federal banking laws. That may be true. But the argument appears to beg the question whether federal laws or state laws should be changed (see chapter 9 for the fallacy of begging the question), or, at a minimum, the argument is weak, since the author does not prove any of the statements made in this paragraph through reliance on any facts or studies.

8.10. a. Paragraph 1 sets forth the immediate political context for the author's argument, namely, that legislation effecting the federal deregulation of marijuana is before the House of Representatives and will be voted on soon. The author also states that other bills reforming federal marijuana regulation are under consideration by the House. In paragraph 8, the author refers very generally to the political context of existing state laws to argue that the rescheduling of marijuana under federal law is not an adequate reform. In paragraph 9, the author refers, again very generally, to the political context of the circumstances in which federal marijuana regulation began (first two sentences) and the adverse effects of that regulation over many decades, up to the present (third sentence).

b. The immediate political context set forth in paragraph 1 in effect says, "My argument is timely; the House of Representatives should act to get the federal government out of the business of regulating marijuana within the next few days." The context provided by the statements in paragraph 8 does not add any meaning that is not expressly stated by those statements themselves.

The historical-political context provided by paragraph 9 (first two sentences) suggests that the initial regulatory laws were ill-considered; that context is suggestive of additional arguments the author could have made, but because this thought is not developed, it only weakly reinforces the arguments he does make. So, too, with the third sentence of paragraph 9; it refers to the adverse social effects of federal regulation over decades, but is only vaguely suggestive of additional arguments the author could have made to support his thesis.

Consider how the author's inductive argument would have been stronger and far more rhetorically powerful if he placed his argument by analogy within the political and social contexts suggested by paragraph 9. In other words, suppose he took the thoughts he quickly touches on in paragraph 9 and moved them near the beginning of the article (say, in paragraph 1 or 2) to set a context for his arguments for deregulation. Then the introductory paragraphs would have proceeded along these lines: (i) federal regulation of marijuana began with the slap-dash and ill-informed action of Congress in 1937, (ii) for many decades that regulation has resulted in great individual harms and social costs, and (iii) Congress now has a chance to correct that mistake and enact sensible legislation getting the federal government out of regulating marijuana. The argument by analogy to alcohol would follow.

c. In view of the number of states that recently have decriminalized the medicinal and/or recreational uses of marijuana and have adopted their own regulatory schemes for marijuana, one might reasonably expect the author to point to those states and use their experiences to support his thesis. It is not as if he is arguing for federal deregulation in a legal-political context in which no states have decriminalized marijuana or implemented their own state regulatory schemes. If those states' experiences with regulation have been generally favorable and have avoided some or all of the problems with federal regulation, the author's argument would be strengthened considerably by relying on such data and facts.

Case Study for Experts: A Book Review by H.L. Mencken

8.12. Number 5 is a *general* statement supported by the *particular* statements in the subpoints. The same is true for numbers 6, 7, and 10. Sometimes you will see the argument proceeding in the opposite way—reasoning from many particular points to a more general point, stated as a conclusion or a preliminary conclusion. That is common when the author is making an inductive argument.

8.13. Numbers 2, 3, 4, and 5 appear to support the proposition that Cleveland was "self-sufficient," that is, he was not manipulated by others and was independent from others in his decision making. Yet the statement in number 5.a that "he stood immovable" is more closely related to the concept of steadfastness, which Mencken does not introduce until paragraph 2 of his essay. One way to reconcile this is to say that my number 5.a should be a major point, a new number 6 illustrating steadfastness. But then there is the issue that my number 5.b (which comes next in the text, at the end of paragraph 1) relates more to self-sufficiency than it does to steadfastness. In short, Mencken seems to be bouncing around with his discussion of self-sufficiency and steadfastness, and does not carefully sort out these two concepts or his evidence for them.

8.14. Before you reach a judgment as to the relevance, or lack of relevance, of number 7 and its subpoints, consider the nature of the thesis Mencken is trying to establish. Mencken's essay is an attempt to argue for a broad and ambiguous value judgment (a normative statement), that is, that Cleveland had the most "solid" and "admirable" character of any president since Washington.

What is a "solid" and "admirable" character? Neither of those terms has one single, fixed, commonly understood meaning. Is a "solid" and "admirable" person one who lives by the Boy Scout Oath, the Ten Commandments, or the Golden Rule? You could imagine an author arguing that a "solid" and "admirable" person is one who guides his life by one or all of these moral codes. Yet Mencken mentions none of these. So, what does Mencken discuss in trying to show that Cleveland had a "solid" and "admirable" character? Why does he discuss the character traits he does and not some others?

In each of the principal statements following his thesis, Mencken is not only trying to support that thesis, but also to give it a more concrete meaning—to tell us what character traits make up a "solid" and "admirable" person. Mencken tells us that a "solid" and "admirable" person is one who can make decisions unfettered by obligations to others, who is not manipulated by others, who holds fast to his decisions and pursues them regardless of political opposition or consequences, and who is motivated primarily by a sense of duty.

In addition to these traits, paragraphs 3 and 4 apparently are intended to bolster Mencken's thesis by showing how Cleveland's "steadfastness" was thoroughly part of his character and not learned through or softened by the fine arts and culture. Paragraph 3 in particular is somewhat critical of Cleveland, painting him as an average bloke who admired other average guys and whose mind was never influenced by any literature or men who may have made his character more nuanced or flexible. The result was that Cleveland was "all his days a somewhat stodgy and pedantic fellow." Mencken's reference to those traits, at a minimum, is consistent with Cleveland's "steadfastness" and Mencken may intend them to further illustrate and give meaning to that term. A person who is steadfast as a matter of character is less likely to be shaken from a decision than a person whose steadfastness is learned and can be unlearned. So, rather than number 7 and its subpoints in the outline stating claims that are irrelevant to or inconsistent with Mencken's thesis, on the reading I am suggesting here, they provide further support for that thesis.

8.15. Each of these three readings is reasonable. The statement in number 10 of my outline may be intended to be part of the argument and to support the thesis because it reinforces Mencken's conclusion about a historical politician by contrasting him with current and future politicians. Alternatively, Mencken may intend this statement to be an implication of his prior argument, a conclusion to be drawn from his argument regarding the uniqueness of Cleveland's character. In other words, Mencken is in effect saying, "if you accept my premises and thesis regarding Cleveland, you should *also* accept this additional conclusion—'It is unlikely that we shall see a President or politician with Cleveland's virtues again.'" In addition to these two alternatives, this third reading is also reasonable—number 10 is a prediction about the future, whereas everything in the argument prior to it is historical. So perhaps Mencken does not intend the statement in number 10 to be part of or implied by his argument; maybe he is just speculating about the future. If you adopt this third reading, then the statement in number 10 (and its subpoints) would be another example of a part of an argumentative text that communicates meaning, but not meaning that is part of or that follows from the argument itself.

8.16. Remember that Mencken's essay is both an argument about President Cleveland's character and a book review. The statement in number 12 is not relevant to Mencken's argument; it is not relevant to stating or proving his thesis. But it does reflect Mencken's purpose of reviewing Dr. Nevins' biography of Cleveland. Accordingly, it is included in the outline and should be included in your outline.

In brief, as you learned in chapter 6 of Reading, the points of your outline may or may not be precisely the same as the thesis (conclusion) and premises of an author's argument. Numbers 10, 11, and 12 in the outline in the text in chapter 8 above state propositions that arguably do not support Mencken's thesis and premises, and, further, they show that those propositions are unrelated to the argument in different ways. Because they are important parts of his essay, they should be included in a complete outline of that essay.

8.17. A very general restatement of his argument may look like this:

President Grover Cleveland made his decisions with self-sufficiency (uninfluenced and not manipulated by others). [Premise]
Once he decided, no matter what the reactions of politicians and the people, he was steadfast (unwavering) in his course of action. [Premise]
No President since Washington was similarly self-sufficient and steadfast. [Premise]
Cleveland's self-sufficiency and steadfastness reflect (are part of) a solid and admirable character. [Premise]

> Therefore, since George Washington, the United States has not had a President whose character was more solid or more admirable than President Cleveland's. [Conclusion]

A more detailed restatement may look like this:

> More than any other President since George Washington, President Grover Cleveland (a) made his decisions independently of the influence of others, (b) was "steadfast" as a matter of character, and (c) was principally motivated by a sense of duty that was an outgrowth of his Calvinistic beliefs, which guided his decisions before any need to be popular. [Premise]
> A "self-sufficient man" is one who makes his decisions independently of the influence of others. [Premise]
> A "steadfast" man is one who, as a matter of character, rigidly (with "no give in him") sticks to his decisions even when challenged by his enemies. [Premise]
> Compared to Cleveland, the three presidents since Washington who are widely regarded as great, namely, Lincoln, Theodore Roosevelt, and Woodrow Wilson, were not as self-sufficient or steadfast. [Premise]
> A "solid" and "admirable" president is one who (a) is a "self-sufficient man," (b) is "steadfast" as a matter of character, and (c) is principally motivated by a sense of duty, even before a need to be popular. [Implied premise]
> Therefore, at least since George Washington, the United States has not had a president whose fundamental character was more solid or more admirable than President Cleveland's. [Conclusion]

It is difficult to restate Mencken's argument precisely. From the perspective of argumentation, this essay is flawed in many ways. His paragraphs contain more than one idea. He uses vague and ambiguous terms like "self-sufficient" (paragraph 1) and then illustrates the meaning of the term with language that appears to better illustrate "steadfastness" (which he does not introduce until paragraph 2), and which itself is ambiguous. He includes paragraphs whose relation to the argument is not entirely clear. And so on. All that said, after trying to restate his argument, you undoubtedly came away from this exercise with a far greater understanding of what Mencken intended to communicate in this essay and how he does so.

8.18. Social and political context may assist the reader in answering the question what *motivated* Mencken to write this essay in the first place. One way to read the essay is that Mencken wrote this book review focusing on the virtues of President Cleveland to make a statement about the moral laxity of recent occupants of the presidency (*e.g.*, President Harding) and the weakness of character of American presidents generally that allows them to be manipulated by special interests. But these types of context do not add much, if any, additional meaning to the essay. Its meaning appears to be entirely communicated by the structure and content of the essay itself.

CHAPTER 9. THE ABC'S OF LOGIC

Exercises

9.1.   a. *Ad hominem*

b. Begging the question

c. Ambiguity/equivocation

d. Begging the question

e. Argument from ignorance and begging the question

f. Ambiguity/equivocation. As literally stated, Americans never stop thinking about ways to harm America. What the President meant is that Americans never stop thinking about ways our enemies might harm America.

g. Begging the question.

h. *Ad hominem*

i. *Non sequitur*

j. Ambiguity/equivocation. It could mean: (a) Smith was walking the dog and in possession of "my binoculars," (b) Smith was walking the dog and the dog had "my binoculars," or (c) the speaker saw Smith walking the dog by using his own (the speaker's) binoculars.

k. One reasonable interpretation of this statement is this: I am right about Cleveland; this truth about Cleveland's character is not widely known because our educational system is poor. On this interpretation, Mencken may be making an *ad hominem* argument by appealing to the special circumstances of his readers. He may be implying something to this effect, "if you, reader, do not know the truth about Cleveland's character, it is because you are poorly educated; and if you were better educated (and knew the history I know), you would agree with my views on Cleveland."

9.2   a. Water is a necessary condition for human life.

b. For a few weeks, food is not a necessary condition for human life.

c. Water, food, and oxygen are jointly necessary and sufficient conditions for human life to survive.

d. Being an unmarried man is a sufficient condition for John to be a bachelor. And, John's being a bachelor is a necessary condition for John's being an unmarried man.

e. Being a bachelor is a sufficient condition for John to be an unmarried man. And, John's being an unmarried man is a necessary condition of his being a bachelor.

Appendix A 105

f. Being the smartest student in the class is a sufficient condition of Mary's being smart (presumably because there are other smart students in the class).

g. You getting a job to pay for books is a necessary condition of my (the speaker's) paying your tuition next semester.

h. Ian's being John's son is a sufficient condition of John being a father.

i. Beatrice being Ian's mother is a necessary condition of Ian being Beatrice's son.

j. The meaning of these two statements, considered together, is ambiguous.

First, they could make the following (silly) statement:

Because they didn't read, the dinosaurs are extinct (did not survive).

This has the form of:

If not X, then not Y.

Which, as you learned, is always logically equivalent to:

If Y, then X.

The dinosaurs would have survived only if they had read.

Or,

If the dinosaurs survived, then they read.

And that is to say (falsely) that reading was a necessary condition of the survival of the dinosaurs.

Second, these statements may be committing a humorous *non sequitur*. Whether or not the dinosaurs read is entirely irrelevant to whether or not they survived, but the (silly and fallacious) statement is that if you want to live (a long time), then you should read.

Third, these sentences do not express either a necessary or a sufficient condition, but rather express a (bad and humorous) causal explanation—not reading causes extinction.

Or, finally, the two sentences may not be making an argument at all. They may just be two sentences placed next to each other, with no implied conclusion. They are no more an argument than this: "I didn't study for the test. I can't jump over skyscrapers."

9.3. The term "indispensable" is a synonym for "necessary." So, the author is stating that "breaking up the concentration of wealth and economic power of corporations" is necessary to producing widespread prosperity. It is a necessary condition. Importantly, the author is also stating that this policy (or action) is *not* a sufficient condition for widespread prosperity, because "it would *not by itself* produce widespread prosperity."

9.4. This sentence can be restated in "If X, then Y" form like this:

If a law is inflicted on a minority that, as a result of being denied the right to vote, had no part in enacting or devising the law, then the law is unjust.

Now the necessary and sufficient conditions should be clearer. Dr. King is saying that for a law to be unjust, it is sufficient that "a law is inflicted on a minority that, as a result of being denied the right to vote, had no part in enacting or devising the law" is true. And he is stating that "the law is unjust" is necessarily true if "a law is inflicted on a minority that, as a result of being denied the right to vote, had no part in enacting or devising the law" is true. In other words, there is no way for "a law is inflicted on a minority that, as a result of being denied the right to vote, had no part in enacting or devising the law" is true and "the law is unjust" is false.

As written and read literally, Dr. King's statement allows no exceptions. It commits him to the position that even a law that gave the nonvoting minority the right to vote would be unjust. And it commits him to the position that a law that lifted all of the nonvoting minority out of extreme poverty is unjust. Once you understand the scope and commitments of this statement, you are then in a position to consider whether Dr. King's rhetoric commits him to a position that is overly broad or too categorical.

9.5. The sentence is stating that "determined legal and nonviolent pressure" is a necessary condition of making any gain in civil rights. The sentence is not stating that "determined legal and nonviolent pressure" is a sufficient condition of making any gain in civil rights, since Dr. King leaves open the possibility that something else also may be needed to make any such gain.

9.6. Because action may not always bring happiness, he is saying that action is *not* a sufficient condition of (action alone will not always bring) happiness. On the other hand, because Disraeli believes that you cannot be happy without action, he is saying that action is a necessary condition of happiness.

9.7. The sentence is ambiguous. It could mean: (a) that equality of opportunity is a necessary condition for social justice (and that if there is social justice, that is sufficient to know that there is equality of opportunity) or (b) that equality of opportunity is a sufficient condition of social justice.

9.8. This statement is ambiguous. It could mean that justice is a necessary condition of peace. Or it could mean that justice is a sufficient condition for peace to exist. Even though the sentence has the "If . . . , then . . ." form (which generally means that whatever is before the "then" is the sufficient condition and whatever follows the "then" is the necessary condition), the author may mean, "if we achieve justice, then we will have peace." In other words, she may mean that justice is a sufficient condition of peace.

9.9. Because this sentence has the "if X, then Y" form, it may look like everything after the "if" is a sufficient condition and everything after the "then" is a necessary condition. But that is not what the writer is really saying, is it? She is not saying that it is necessary to start a nuclear war to kill 100 million people in an hour, is she? Of course not. The author may believe the sentence in our example and also believe that there are many other ways to kill 100 million people in an hour (such as using massive, widespread chemical warfare). Rather, she is saying "starting a nuclear war" is sufficient to kill 100 million people in an hour. That is the meaning of the phrase "all they need to do . . ." In other words, she means, "If the leaders of the superpowers start a nuclear war, that's all they need to do (or, that would be sufficient) to kill 100 million people in an hour." So, "the leaders of the superpowers starting a nuclear war" is the sufficient condition.

Exercises for Extra Study

9.10. You could restate it like this:

If everyone had a good, meaningful job, then we would solve the opioid crisis.

In other words, the writer is saying that "everyone having a good, meaningful job" is a sufficient condition of "solving the opioid crisis." If "everyone having a good, meaningful job" is true, that is sufficient for "solving the opioid crisis" to be true.

9.11. a. You can paraphrase it like this:

If a person lives a moral life, then she recognizes that we are all fundamentally interconnected.

Or like this:

A person will live a moral life only if she recognizes that we are all fundamentally interconnected.

b. The necessary condition in my restatements is: she recognizes that we are all fundamentally interconnected.

c. The sufficient condition is: "A person living a moral life" (the truth of "Jane is living a moral life" is sufficient for "Jane recognizes that we are all fundamentally interconnected" to be true).

Recall our discussion of ambiguity in chapter 7 of *Reading*. "Fundamentally interconnected" is ambiguous. If you were to see this phrase in an essay on morality, you would want to examine that essay to see what reasonable meanings it may have and which of those the author may intend.

9.12. This sentence could be restated as:

A person is happy only if he is stupid, selfish, and has good health.

Here we have a statement that three things as a set or group are the necessary condition. "Being stupid, selfish, and having good health" are, as a group, the necessary condition of being happy and if it is true that a person is happy, that is sufficient for the truth of the statement that "he is stupid, selfish, and in good health."

9.13. a. It is "it's cloudy but not raining." Here, we have two things that together are said to be a sufficient condition (just as in the prior exercise we had three things that together were a necessary condition).

b. We cannot say. All that we can conclude for certain from the example is that he thinks that those two conditions jointly are sufficient for catching big fish. Maybe he also thinks that if it is cloudy, raining, and some other condition is added (*e.g.*, you are fishing before 6 a.m.) those three conditions also are jointly sufficient for catching big fish. But we cannot draw that conclusion from what the example says.

You may have noticed that there is something "fishy" going on in this example. When you see the phrase "depends on," as in this example, that typically means something that is necessary, a necessary condition. So Stanley's statement is that the factors (conditions) he has stated are necessary to catching big fish. But the person who disagrees implicitly is taking them to be sufficient conditions, and then stating what he takes to be the correct sufficient conditions. His disagreement misses the point of Stanley's comment. To disagree with Stanley's comment as Stanley presumably intended it, the other person would have to show that Stanley's necessary conditions are not in fact necessary. When two positions speak past each other in this fashion, both could be true.

9.14. a. Try this:

We will have peace on earth only if we recognize that all men and women are brothers and sisters.

So, the necessary condition of having peace on earth is that we recognize that all men and women are brothers and sisters.

b. "We" is such a common, everyday word that we seldom stop and ask what it means. In this sentence "we" might mean everyone in your neighborhood, the entire United States, everyone in countries at war, or *everyone* with no exceptions. If the author means everyone with no exceptions, then the sentence literally means that if just one person does not recognize that all men and women are brothers and sisters, then we will not have peace on earth. That is an incredibly strong position to defend.

What would be a more reasonable interpretation of "we"? Something like, "not literally everyone, but a large majority of people." In that case, the sentence means, "there will be peace on earth only if a large majority of people accepts the truth that we are all brothers and sisters."

9.15. Like this:

If you are growing (spiritually), then you have suffered (or are suffering).

Or,

If you have grown (spiritually), then you have suffered.

As these alternative restatements indicate, the sentence is ambiguous as to past or future tense.

9.16. No. The author is not saying that being an artist, actor, politician, or intellectual is a necessary condition of suffering from depression; in fact, he is stating just the opposite in the last sentence. Neither is the author stating that being an artist, actor, politician, or intellectual is a sufficient condition of suffering from depression. He is not stating that if you are one of these, then that is sufficient for you to suffer from depression. Not everything is a necessary or a sufficient condition.

9.17. The second sentence answers the question. It says that concentration is a necessary, but not a sufficient, condition of being a better reader.

9.18. To rephrase this sentence, he is saying something to this effect, "it's always raining in Seattle, so if it is not raining, then we know we are not in Seattle." And that sentence has the same meaning as this:

If we're in Seattle, then it's raining.

The truth of "we're in Seattle" is sufficient to know that "it's raining" is true, and "it's raining" being true is a necessary condition for "we're in Seattle" to be true (since your friend thinks it is always raining in Seattle).

Recall the rule of thumb—any time you see a "if not X, then not Y" sentence, you can flip the position of X and Y and get rid of the two "nots" and the sentence will have the same logical meaning, and it often will be easier to figure out the necessary and sufficient conditions.

By the same token, you can take any "if X, then Y" statement, and flip the X and Y, and add "not" before each of them and get a sentence with the same meaning. Try that with some of the examples we have considered above.

Extra Exercises for Experts

9.19.   a. Valid. *Modus ponens.*

b. Invalid. Affirming the consequent.

c. Invalid. Affirming the consequent.

d. Invalid. Denying the antecedent.

e. Invalid. Affirming the consequent. The first premise says that breaking up concentrated wealth and power is a necessary condition of creating prosperity. That statement does not say that is sufficient to create widespread prosperity.

f. Valid. *Modus tollens.*

g. Invalid. Denying the antecedent. A person may believe that the concentration of wealth and power is unjust, independent of its effect on prosperity. So, he may still think it necessary to break up concentrated wealth and power for reasons of justice and not for reasons of spreading prosperity.

Appendix B

Refugees Don't Undermine the US Economy—They Energize It

Ramya Vijaya, Professor of Economics, Stockton University

Reprinted from *The Conversation*, available at, Refugees don't undermine the US economy – they energize it (theconversation.com)

The Trump administration last month announced plans to cut the number of refugees allowed to enter the United States to the lowest level in 40 years. This year's cap of 18,000 admissions is well below the average annual limit of about 95,000 refugees in the years before the Trump administration.

This drastic cut typifies the Trump administration's overall anti-immigration stance, reflected in a series of executive orders aimed at reducing undocumented and legal migration channels in the past four years.

The administration has said that refugees—those forced to leave their country to escape war or persecution—do not benefit the U.S. economy. It has portrayed refugees as a drain on resources and argued that a lower number of refugees is required to prioritize the well-being of Americans.

This feeds into the perception among some Americans that immigrants come to this country and either take their jobs or do not work at all and live off of welfare. Both those ideas are false.

In my research, I have found that refugees are far from an economic drain. They are quick to integrate into local economies. And nationally they have high labor force participation rates, which includes people who are employed or looking for employment.

Government backing

The U.S. resettlement program began in 1980 with the Refugee Act, passed with unanimous bipartisan support. The measure established the formal mechanism for refugee resettlement in the country, including an Office of Refugee Resettlement within the State Department.

The program gives money to help often destitute refugees resettle—roughly $2,000 per refugee, not including local-level resources that vary per state—to assist with living expenses for the first three months upon arrival. For further assistance, refugees can apply for programs like welfare or food stamps.

Those who do not qualify for welfare can apply for the Refugee Cash Assistance program. The amount of assistance varies by state but is usually in the range of $300 a month. RCA in Washington state, for example, is capped at $363 per individual per month. This assistance is available to refugees for up to eight months from their arrival date.

A major focus of the resettlement process, however, is to encourage refugees to achieve economic independence quickly.

Within a month of arrival, refugees receive permission to work legally. During the first eight months, the program also provides language training and employment support services.

An economic success

After analyzing State Department data as well as U.S. Census data, I've found that refugees have integrated well into U.S. labor markets despite arriving from vastly different backgrounds—the top five countries of birth were Burma, Iraq, Somalia, Bhutan and Sudan.

From the Census data, I found that 64% of refugee women who have spent 10 years or more in the U.S. are working or actively looking for work, compared with 55% for native-born women. This is true even after controlling for individual characteristics like age, level of education and English proficiency.

Local-level success

I also found similar trends at the local level. Using the same Census data, I compared refugees resettled in Philadelphia, Pennsylvania, with the local population.

I found that the median household income estimates for refugees resettled in the area for seven or more years was $46,126, higher than the median income estimate of $38,253 for the local population.

And 66% of refugees in Philadelphia were working or looking for work, compared with the local average of 56%. While newly arriving refugees have low levels of English proficiency, after seven years nearly 76% report English fluency.

Other studies report similar findings across the country.

An economic impact study in Cleveland found that refugee families made substantial economic contributions to the region, leading to an estimated $48 million in additional spending in 2012. As the study notes, refugees typically found employment within five months of being resettled.

Several other cities have seen economic revitalization due to refugee resettlement. Due to an influx of refugees, Utica and Buffalo, New York, were able to reverse long-term population decline. Successive groups of refugees revived neighborhoods in these shrinking cities, expanded the tax base and set up small businesses.

Nationally, I also found that refugees find the kind of jobs deemed essential services during the coronavirus pandemic. The top occupational categories for refugee women include housekeeping, nursing and home health care aides. Refugee men are often hired as meat and fish processors or janitors.

Many Americans argue that refugee resettlement is a moral obligation. But it's also worth reiterating that often the opposition to refugee resettlement is based on a misperception about the economics.

Reprinted with the kind permission of the author and The Conversation *under a Creative Commons Attribution/No derivatives license.*

Appendix C
The Disadvantages of an Elite Education
William Deresiewicz

The complete, original article was published in the *American Scholar*, June 1, 2008, and is available at, https://theamericanscholar.org/the-disadvantages-of-an-elite-education/#.XkQa7Y3saQU

It didn't dawn on me that there might be a few holes in my education until I was about 35. I'd just bought a house, the pipes needed fixing, and the plumber was standing in my kitchen. There he was, a short, beefy guy with a goatee and a Red Sox cap and a thick Boston accent, and I suddenly learned that I didn't have the slightest idea what to say to someone like him. So alien was his experience to me, so unguessable his values, so mysterious his very language, that I couldn't succeed in engaging him in a few minutes of small talk before he got down to work. Fourteen years of higher education and a handful of Ivy League degrees, and there I was, stiff and stupid, struck dumb by my own dumbness. "Ivy retardation," a friend of mine calls this. I could carry on conversations with people from other countries, in other languages, but I couldn't talk to the man who was standing in my own house.

It's not surprising that it took me so long to discover the extent of my miseducation, because the last thing an elite education will teach you is its own inadequacy. As two dozen years at Yale and Columbia have shown me, elite colleges relentlessly encourage their students to flatter themselves for being there, and for what being there can do for them. The advantages of an elite education are indeed undeniable. You learn to think, at least in certain ways, and you make the contacts needed to launch yourself into a life rich in all of society's most cherished rewards. To consider that while some opportunities are being created, others are being cancelled and that while some abilities are being developed, others are being crippled is, within this context, not only outrageous, but inconceivable.

I'm not talking about curricula or the culture wars, the closing or opening of the American mind, political correctness, canon formation, or what have you. I'm talking about the whole system in which these skirmishes play out. Not just the Ivy League and its peer institutions, but also the mechanisms that get you there in the first place: the private and affluent public "feeder" schools, the ever-growing parastructure of tutors and test-prep courses and enrichment programs, the whole admissions frenzy and everything that leads up to and away from it. The message, as always, is the medium. Before, after, and around the elite college classroom, a constellation of values is ceaselessly inculcated. As globalization sharpens economic insecurity, we are increasingly committing ourselves—as students, as parents, as a society—to a vast apparatus of educational advantage. With so many resources devoted to the business of elite academics and so many people scrambling for the limited space at the top of the ladder, it is worth asking what exactly it is you get in the end—what it is we all get, because the elite students of today, as their institutions never tire of reminding them, are the leaders of tomorrow.

The first disadvantage of an elite education, as I learned in my kitchen that day, is that it makes you incapable of talking to people who aren't like you. Elite schools pride themselves on their diversity, but that diversity is almost entirely a matter of ethnicity and race. With respect to class, these schools are largely—indeed increasingly—homogeneous. Visit any elite campus in our great nation and you can thrill to the heartwarming spectacle of the children of white businesspeople and professionals studying and playing alongside the children of black, Asian, and Latino businesspeople and professionals. At the same time, because these schools tend to cultivate liberal attitudes, they leave their students in the paradoxical position of wanting to advocate on behalf of the working class while being unable to hold a simple conversation with anyone in it. Witness the last two Democratic presidential nominees, Al Gore and John Kerry: one each from Harvard and Yale, both earnest, decent, intelligent men, both utterly incapable of communicating with the larger electorate.

But it isn't just a matter of class. My education taught me to believe that people who didn't go to an Ivy League or equivalent school weren't worth talking to, regardless of their class. I was given the unmistakable message that such people were beneath me. We were "the best and the brightest," as these places love to say, and everyone else was, well, something else: less good, less bright.... I never learned that there are smart people who don't go to elite colleges, often precisely for reasons of class. I never learned that there are smart people who don't go to college at all.

I also never learned that there are smart people who aren't "smart." The existence of multiple forms of intelligence has become a commonplace, but however much elite universities like to sprinkle their incoming classes with a few actors or violinists, they select for and develop one form of intelligence:

the analytic. While this is broadly true of all universities, elite schools, precisely because their students (and faculty, and administrators) possess this one form of intelligence to such a high degree, are more apt to ignore the value of others. . . . But social intelligence and emotional intelligence and creative ability, to name just three other forms, are not distributed preferentially among the educational elite. The "best" are the brightest only in one narrow sense. . . .

What about people who aren't bright in any sense? I have a friend who went to an Ivy League college after graduating from a typically mediocre public high school. One of the values of going to such a school, she once said, is that it teaches you to relate to stupid people. Some people are smart in the elite-college way, some are smart in other ways, and some aren't smart at all. It should be embarrassing not to know how to talk to any of them, if only because talking to people is the only real way of knowing them. Elite institutions are supposed to provide a humanistic education, but the first principle of humanism is Terence's: "nothing human is alien to me." The first disadvantage of an elite education is how very much of the human it alienates you from.

The second disadvantage, implicit in what I've been saying, is that an elite education inculcates a false sense of self-worth. Getting to an elite college, being at an elite college, and going on from an elite college—all involve numerical rankings: SAT, GPA, GRE. You learn to think of yourself in terms of those numbers. They come to signify not only your fate, but your identity; not only your identity, but your value. It's been said that what those tests really measure is your ability to take tests, but even if they measure something real, it is only a small slice of the real. The problem begins when students are encouraged to forget this truth, when academic excellence becomes excellence in some absolute sense, when "better at X" becomes simply "better."

There is nothing wrong with taking pride in one's intellect or knowledge. There is something wrong with the smugness and self-congratulation that elite schools connive at from the moment the fat envelopes come in the mail. From orientation to graduation, the message is implicit in every tone of voice and tilt of the head, every old-school tradition, every article in the student paper, every speech from the dean. The message is: You have arrived. Welcome to the club. And the corollary is equally clear: You deserve everything your presence here is going to enable you to get. When people say that students at elite schools have a strong sense of entitlement, they mean that those students think they deserve more than other people because their SAT scores are higher.

At Yale, and no doubt at other places, the message is reinforced in embarrassingly literal terms. The physical form of the university—its quads and residential colleges, with their Gothic stone façades and wrought-iron portals—is constituted by the locked gate set into the encircling wall. . . . The gate, in other words, is a kind of governing metaphor—because the social form of the university, as is true of every elite school, is constituted the same way. Elite colleges are walled domains guarded by locked gates, with admission granted only to the elect. . . .

One of the great errors of an elite education, then, is that it teaches you to think that measures of intelligence and academic achievement are measures of value in some moral or metaphysical sense. But they're not. Graduates of elite schools are not more valuable than stupid people, or talentless people, or even lazy people. Their pain does not hurt more. Their souls do not weigh more. If I were religious, I would say, God does not love them more. The political implications should be clear. As John Ruskin told an older elite, grabbing what you can get isn't any less wicked when you grab it with the power of your brains than with the power of your fists. . . .

The political implications don't stop there. An elite education not only ushers you into the upper classes; it trains you for the life you will lead once you get there. I didn't understand this until I began comparing my experience, and even more, my students' experience, with the experience of a friend of mine who went to Cleveland State. There are due dates and attendance requirements at places like Yale, but no one takes them very seriously. Extensions are available for the asking; threats to deduct credit for missed classes are rarely, if ever, carried out. In other words, students at places like Yale get an endless string of second chances. Not so at places like Cleveland State. My friend once got a D in a class in which she'd been running an A because she was coming off a waitressing shift and had to hand in her term paper an hour late.

That may be an extreme example, but it is unthinkable at an elite school. Just as unthinkably, she had no one to appeal to. Students at places like Cleveland State, unlike those at places like Yale, don't have a platoon of advisers and tutors and deans to write out excuses for late work, give them extra help when they need it, pick them up when they fall down. They get their education wholesale, from an indifferent bureaucracy; it's not handed to them in individually wrapped packages by smiling clerks. There are few, if any, opportunities for the kind of contacts I saw my students get routinely—classes with visiting power brokers, dinners with foreign dignitaries. . . .

Students at places like Cleveland State also don't get A–'s just for doing the work. There's been a lot of handwringing lately over grade inflation, and it is a scandal, but the most scandalous thing about it is how uneven it's been. Forty years ago, the average GPA at both public and private universities was about 2.6, still close to the traditional B–/C+ curve. Since then, it's gone up everywhere, but not by anything like the same amount. The average GPA at public universities is now about 3.0, a B; at private universities it's about 3.3, just short of a B+. And at most Ivy League schools, it's closer to 3.4. But there are always students who don't do the work, or who are taking a class far outside their field (for fun or to fulfill a requirement), or who aren't up to standard to begin with (athletes, legacies). At a school like Yale, students who come to class and work hard expect nothing less than an A–. And most of the time, they get it.

In short, the way students are treated in college trains them for the social position they will occupy once they get out. At schools like Cleveland State, they're being trained for positions somewhere in the middle of the class system, in the depths of one bureaucracy or another. They're being conditioned for lives with few second chances, no extensions, little support, narrow opportunity—lives of subordination, supervision, and control, lives of deadlines, not guidelines. At places like Yale, of course, it's the reverse. The elite like to think of themselves as belonging to a meritocracy, but that's true only up to a point. Getting through the gate is very difficult, but once you're in, there's almost nothing you can do to get kicked out. Not the most abject academic failure, not the most heinous act of plagiarism, not even threatening a fellow student with bodily harm—I've heard of all three—will get you expelled. The feeling is that, by gosh, it just wouldn't be fair—in other words, the self-protectiveness of the old-boy network, even if it now includes girls. Elite schools nurture excellence, but they also nurture what a former Yale graduate student I know calls "entitled mediocrity." A is the mark of excellence; A– is the mark of entitled mediocrity. . . .

Here, too, college reflects the way things work in the adult world (unless it's the other way around). For the elite, there's always another extension—a bailout, a pardon, a stint in rehab—always plenty of contacts and special stipends—the country club, the conference, the year-end bonus, the dividend. If Al Gore and John Kerry represent one of the characteristic products of an elite education, George W. Bush represents another. It's no coincidence that our current president, the apotheosis of entitled mediocrity, went to Yale. Entitled mediocrity is indeed the operating principle of his administration, but as Enron and WorldCom and the other scandals of the dot-com meltdown demonstrated, it's also the operating principle of corporate America. The fat salaries paid to underperforming CEOs are an adult version of the A–. . . .

If one of the disadvantages of an elite education is the temptation it offers to mediocrity, another is the temptation it offers to security. When parents explain why they work so hard to give their children the best possible education, they invariably say it is because of the opportunities it opens up. But what of the opportunities it shuts down? An elite education gives you the chance to be rich—which is, after all, what we're talking about—but it takes away the chance not to be. Yet the opportunity not to be rich is one of the greatest opportunities with which young Americans have been blessed. We live in a society that is itself so wealthy that it can afford to provide a decent living to whole classes of people who in other countries exist (or in earlier times existed) on the brink of poverty or, at least, of indignity. You can live comfortably in the United States as a schoolteacher, or a community organizer, or a civil rights lawyer, or an artist—that is, by any reasonable definition of comfort. You have to live in an ordinary house instead of an apartment in Manhattan or a mansion in L.A.; you have to drive a Honda instead of a BMW or a Hummer; you have to vacation in Florida instead of Barbados or Paris, but what are such losses when set against the opportunity to do work you believe in, work you're suited for, work you love, every day of your life?

Yet it is precisely that opportunity that an elite education takes away. How can I be a schoolteacher—wouldn't that be a waste of my expensive education? Wouldn't I be squandering the opportunities my parents worked so hard to provide? What will my friends think? . . . And the question that lies behind all these: Isn't it beneath me? So a whole universe of possibility closes, and you miss your true calling.

This is not to say that students from elite colleges never pursue a riskier or less lucrative course after graduation, but even when they do, they tend to give up more quickly than others. . . . This doesn't seem to make sense, especially since students from elite schools tend to graduate with less debt and are more likely to be able to float by on family money for a while. I wasn't aware of the phenomenon myself until I heard about it from a couple of graduate students in my department, one from Yale, one from Harvard. They were talking about trying to write poetry, how friends of theirs from college called it quits within a year or two while people they know from less prestigious schools are still at it. Why should this be? Because students from elite schools expect success, and expect it now. They have, by definition, never experienced anything else, and their sense of self has been built around their ability to succeed. The idea of not being successful terrifies them, disorients them, defeats them. They've been driven their whole lives by a fear of failure. . . .

But if you're afraid to fail, you're afraid to take risks, which begins to explain the final and most damning disadvantage of an elite education: that it is profoundly anti-intellectual. This will seem counterintuitive. Aren't kids at elite schools the smartest ones around, at least in the narrow academic sense? Don't they work harder than anyone else—indeed, harder than any previous generation? They are. They do. But being an intellectual is not the same as being smart. Being an intellectual means more than doing your homework.

If so few kids come to college understanding this, it is no wonder. They are products of a system that rarely asked them to think about something bigger than the next assignment. The system forgot to teach them, along the way to the prestige admissions and the lucrative jobs, that the most important achievements can't be measured by a letter or a number or a name. It forgot that the true purpose of education is to make minds, not careers.

Being an intellectual means, first of all, being passionate about ideas—and not just for the duration of a semester, for the sake of pleasing the teacher, or for getting a good grade. A friend who teaches at the University of Connecticut once complained to me that his students don't think for themselves. Well, I said, Yale students think for themselves, but only because they know we want them to. . . . Places like Yale, as one of [my students] put it to me, are not conducive to searchers.

Places like Yale are simply not set up to help students ask the big questions. I don't think there ever was a golden age of intellectualism in the American university, but in the 19th century students might at least have had a chance to hear such questions raised in chapel or in the literary societies and debating clubs that flourished on campus. Throughout much of the 20th century, with the growth of the humanistic ideal in American colleges, students might have encountered the big questions in the classrooms of professors possessed of a strong sense of pedagogic mission. Teachers like that still exist in this country, but the increasingly dire exigencies of academic professionalization have made them all but extinct at elite universities. Professors at top research institutions are valued exclusively for the quality of their scholarly work; time spent on teaching is time lost. . . .

When elite universities boast that they teach their students how to think, they mean that they teach them the analytic and rhetorical skills necessary for success in law or medicine or science or business. But a humanistic education is supposed to mean something more than that, as universities still dimly feel. So when students get to college, they hear a couple of speeches telling them to ask the big questions, and when they graduate, they hear a couple more speeches telling them to ask the big questions. And in between, they spend four years taking courses that train them to ask the little questions—specialized courses, taught by specialized professors, aimed at specialized students. Although the notion of breadth is implicit in the very idea of a liberal arts education, the admissions process increasingly selects for kids who have already begun to think of themselves in specialized terms—the junior journalist, the budding astronomer, the language prodigy. We are slouching, even at elite schools, toward a glorified form of vocational training.

Indeed, that seems to be exactly what those schools want. There's a reason elite schools speak of training leaders, not thinkers—holders of power, not its critics. An independent mind is independent of all allegiances, and elite schools, which get a large percentage of their budget from alumni giving, are strongly invested in fostering institutional loyalty. As another friend, a third-generation Yalie, says, the purpose of Yale College is to manufacture Yale alumni. Of course, for the system to work, those alumni need money. At Yale, the long-term drift of students away from majors in the humanities and basic sciences toward more practical ones like computer science and economics has been abetted by administrative indifference. The college career office has little to say to students not interested in law, medicine, or business, and elite universities are not going to do anything to discourage the large percentage of their graduates who take their degrees to Wall Street. In fact, they're showing them the way. . . .

. . .

Yet there is a dimension of the intellectual life that lies above the passion for ideas, though so thoroughly has our culture been sanitized of it that it is hardly surprising if it was beyond the reach of even my most alert students. Since the idea of the intellectual emerged in the 18th century, it has had, at its core, a commitment to social transformation. Being an intellectual means thinking your way toward a vision of the good society and then trying to realize that vision by speaking truth to power. It means going into spiritual exile. It means foreswearing your allegiance, in lonely freedom, to God, to country, and to Yale. It takes more than just intellect; it takes imagination and courage. . . .

Being an intellectual begins with thinking your way outside of your assumptions and the system that enforces them. But students who get into elite schools are precisely the ones who have best learned to work within the system, so it's almost impossible for them to see outside it, to see that it's even there. Long before they got to college, they turned themselves into world-class hoop-jumpers and teacher-pleasers, getting A's in every class no matter how boring they found the teacher or how pointless the subject, racking up eight or 10 extracurricular activities no matter what else they wanted to do with their time. Paradoxically, the situation may be better at second-tier schools and, in particular, again, at liberal arts colleges than at the most prestigious universities. Some students end up at second-tier schools because they're exactly like students at Harvard or Yale, only less gifted or driven. But others end up there because they have a more independent spirit. They didn't get straight A's because they couldn't be bothered to give everything in every class. They concentrated on the ones that meant the most to them or on a single strong extracurricular passion or on projects that had nothing to do with school or even with looking good on a college application. . . .

I've been struck, during my time at Yale, by how similar everyone looks. You hardly see any hippies or punks or art-school types, and at a college that was known in the '80s as the Gay Ivy, few out lesbians and no gender queers. The geeks don't look all that geeky; the fashionable kids go in for understated elegance. Thirty-two flavors, all of them vanilla. The most elite schools have become places of a narrow and suffocating normalcy. Everyone feels pressure to maintain the kind of appearance—and affect—that go with achievement. . . .

I taught a class several years ago on the literature of friendship. One day we were discussing Virginia Woolf's novel *The Waves,* which follows a group of friends from childhood to middle age. In high school, one of them falls in love with another boy. He thinks, "To whom can I expose the urgency of my own passion? . . . There is nobody—here among these grey arches, and moaning pigeons, and cheerful games and tradition and emulation, all so skilfully organised to prevent feeling alone." A pretty good description of an elite college campus, including the part about never being allowed to feel alone. What did my students think of this, I wanted to know? What does it mean to go to school at a place where you're never alone? Well, one of them said, I do feel uncomfortable sitting in my room by myself. Even when I have to write a paper, I do it at a friend's. . . .

. . . There's been much talk of late about the loss of privacy, but equally calamitous is its corollary, the loss of solitude. It used to be that you couldn't always get together with your friends even when you wanted to. Now that students are in constant electronic contact, they never have trouble finding each other. But it's not as if their compulsive sociability is enabling them to develop deep friendships. "To whom can I expose the urgency of my own passion?": my student was in her friend's room writing a paper, not having a heart-to-heart. She probably didn't have the time; indeed, other students told me they found their peers too busy for intimacy.

What happens when busyness and sociability leave no room for solitude? The ability to engage in introspection, I put it to my students that day, is the essential precondition for living an intellectual life, and the essential precondition for introspection is solitude. They took this in for a second, and then one of them said, with a dawning sense of self-awareness, "So are you saying that we're all just, like, really excellent sheep?" Well, I don't know. But I do know that the life of the mind is lived one mind at a time: one solitary, skeptical, resistant mind at a time. The best place to cultivate it is not within an educational system whose real purpose is to reproduce the class system.

The world that produced John Kerry and George Bush is indeed giving us our next generation of leaders. The kid who's loading up on AP courses junior year or editing three campus publications while double-majoring, the kid whom everyone wants at their college or law school but no one wants in their classroom, the kid who doesn't have a minute to breathe, let alone think, will soon be running a corporation or an institution or a government. She will have many achievements but little experience, great success but no vision. The disadvantage of an elite education is that it's given us the elite we have, and the elite we're going to have.

This edited version of "The Disadvantages of an Elite Education" is reprinted with the kind permission, and under license, of William Deresiewicz.

Appendix D
True Meaning of July 4 is Sacrifice
Carl J. Asszony

Reprinted from the *Daily Record* (NJ), July 3, 2018.

The Fourth of July has become another national holiday of great historical significance that will be overshadowed by sales at the mall, barbecues, and other social events. The real meaning of this important date is gradually being forgotten.

On July 4, 1776 the members of the Continental Congress adopted the Declaration of Independence which proclaimed their desire to break away from the oppressive mother country of England and to become a free and independent nation. These men were aware of the dangers and challenges that lay ahead by taking such a bold step. The military conflict with England had begun nearly a year before. Yet, they were willing to continue that struggle, not only in battle, but in words on parchment, "To secure the blessings of liberty to ourselves and prosperity."

With the signing of that declaration they mutually pledged to each other their lives, their fortunes and their sacred honor. These founding fathers would pay a heavy price for putting their names to that extraordinary document.

Five of the signers were captured by the British and tortured. Nine died from wounds in battle, or from the hardships endured during the Revolutionary War. Two lost sons in battle, two other sons were captured and treated brutally. Richard Stockton of New Jersey was arrested, beaten, jailed and so cruelly treated to the point that his health failed and he died before the Revolutionary War ended. His estate was looted and burned. His family had to live off charity for the remainder of their lives. The wife of Francis Lewis was thrown into a dark, damp prison cell without a bed. She died from the effects of confinement. Their son would also die in while in captivity. Carter

Baxter, a trader, lost his ships to the British. He had loaned a great deal of money to the American cause and was never repaid. He was forced to sell his properties to pay his debts. Some of the other signers ended up in poverty or struggled desperately to rebuild their lives. Their homes had been looted, property destroyed and many of the families lived in great hardship.

Frederick Douglass, a former slave, renowned speaker and intellectual, pointed out in a speech given July 5, 1852, that, "The signers of the Declaration of Independence were brave men. It does not often happen to a nation to raise, at one time, such a number of truly great men. They loved their country better than their own private interests; all will concede that is a rare virtue. I will unite with you to honor their memories."

As we go about the July 4th festivities, let us remember that this day is not about hot dogs, beer, shopping and fireworks. It is about celebrating the birth of a nation. A nation that was born, grew and survived through the centuries because of the pain, tears and sacrifices suffered by so many.

Happy Birthday, America.

Reprinted under license. © Daily Record—USA TODAY NETWORK

Appendix E
Antidotes for Fear
Martin Luther King Jr.

There is no fear in love; but perfect love casteth out fear: because fear hath torment. He that feareth is not made perfect in love. I John 4:18

In these days of catastrophic change and calamitous uncertainty, is there any man who does not experience the depression and bewilderment of crippling fear, which, like a nagging hound of hell, pursues our every footstep?

Everywhere men and women are confronted by fears that often appear in strange disguises and a variety of wardrobes. Haunted by the possibility of bad health, we detect in every meaningless symptom an evidence of disease. Troubled by the fact that days and years pass so quickly, we dose ourselves with drugs which promise eternal youth. If we are physically vigorous, we become so concerned by the prospect that our personalities may collapse that we develop an inferiority complex and stumble through life with a feeling of insecurity, a lack of self-confidence, and a sense of impending failure. A fear of what life may bring encourages some persons to wander aimlessly along the frittering road of excessive drink and sexual promiscuity. Almost without being aware of the change, many people have permitted fear to transform the sunrise of love and peace into a sunset of inner depression.

When unchecked, fear spawns a whole brood of phobias—fear of water, high places, closed rooms, darkness, loneliness, among others—and such an accumulation culminates in phobiaphobia or the fear of fear itself.

Especially common in our highly competitive society are economic fears, from which, Karen Horney says, come most of the psychological problems of our age. Captains of industry are tormented by the possible failure of their business and the capriciousness of the stock market. Employees are plagued by the prospect of unemployment and the consequences of an ever-increasing automation.

And consider, too, the multiplication in our day of religious and ontological fears, which include the fear of death and racial annihilation. The advent of the atomic age, which should have ushered in an era of plenty and of prosperity, has lifted the fear of death to morbid proportions. The terrifying spectacle of nuclear warfare has put Hamlet's words, "To be or not to be," on millions of trembling lips. Witness our frenzied efforts to construct fallout shelters. As though even these offer sanctuary from an H-bomb attack! Witness the agonizing desperation of our petitions that our government increase the nuclear stockpile. But our fanatical quest to maintain "a balance of terror" only increases our fear and leaves nations on tiptoes lest some diplomatic *faux pas* ignite a frightful holocaust.

Realizing that fear drains a man's energy and depletes his resources, Emerson wrote, "He has not learned the lesson of life who does not every day surmount a fear."

But I do not mean to suggest that we should seek to eliminate fear altogether from human life. Were this humanly possible, it would be practically undesirable. Fear is the elemental alarm system of the human organism which warns of approaching dangers and without which man could not have survived in either the primitive or modern worlds. Fear, moreover, is a powerfully creative force. Every great invention and intellectual advance represents a desire to escape from some dreaded circumstance or condition. The fear of darkness led to the discovery of the secret of electricity. The fear of pain led to the marvelous advances of medical science. The fear of ignorance was one reason that man built great institutions of learning. The fear of war was one of the forces behind the birth of the United Nations. Angelo Patri has rightly said, "Education consists in being afraid at the right time." If man were to lose his capacity to fear, he would be deprived of his capacity to grow, invent, and create. So in a sense fear is normal, necessary, and creative.

But we must remember that abnormal fears are emotionally ruinous and psychologically destructive. To illustrate the difference between normal and abnormal fear, Sigmund Freud spoke of a person who was quite properly afraid of snakes in the heart of an African jungle and another person who neurotically feared that snakes were under the carpet in his city apartment. Psychologists say that normal children are born with only two fears—the fear of falling and the fear of loud noises—and that all others are environmentally acquired. Most of these acquired fears are snakes under the carpet.

It is to such fears that we usually refer when we speak of getting rid of fear. But this is only a part of the story. Normal fear protects us; abnormal fear paralyzes us. Normal fear motivates us to improve our individual and collective welfare; abnormal fear constantly poisons and distorts our inner lives. Our problem is not to be rid of fear but rather to harness and master it. How may it be mastered?

I

First, we must unflinchingly face our fears and honestly ask ourselves why we are afraid. This confrontation will, to some measure, grant us power. We shall never be cured of fear by escapism or repression, for the more we attempt to ignore and repress our fears, the more we multiply our inner conflicts.

By looking squarely and honestly at our fears we learn that many of them are residues of some childhood need or apprehension. Here, for instance, is a person haunted by a fear of death or the thought of punishment in the afterlife, who discovers that he has unconsciously projected into the whole of reality the childhood experience of being punished by his parents, locked in a room, and seemingly deserted. Or here is a man plagued by the fear of inferiority and social rejection, who discovers that rejection in childhood by a self-centered mother and a preoccupied father left him with a self-defeating sense of inadequacy and a repressed bitterness toward life.

By bringing our fears to the forefront of consciousness, we may find them to be more imaginary than real. Some of them will turn out to be snakes under the carpet.

And let us also remember that, more often than not, fear involves the misuse of the imagination. When we get our fears into the open, we may laugh at some of them, and this is good. One psychiatrist said, "Ridicule is the master cure for fear and anxiety."

II

Second, we can master fear through one of the supreme virtues known to man: courage. Plato considered courage to be an element of the soul which bridges the cleavage between reason and desire. Aristotle thought of courage as the affirmation of man's essential nature. Thomas Aquinas said that courage is the strength of mind capable of conquering whatever threatens the attainment of the highest good.

Courage, therefore, is the power of the mind to overcome fear. Unlike anxiety, fear has a definite object which may be faced, analyzed, attacked, and, if need be, endured. How often the object of our fear is fear itself: In his *Journal* Henry David Thoreau wrote, "Nothing is so much to be feared as fear." Centuries earlier, Epictetus wrote, "For it is not death or hardship that is a fearful thing, but the fear of hardship and death." Courage takes the fear produced by a definite object into itself and thereby conquers the fear involved. Paul Tillich has written, "Courage is self-affirmation 'in spite of' . . . that which tends to hinder the self from affirming itself." It is self-affirmation in spite of death and nonbeing, and he who is courageous takes the fear of death into his self-affirmation and acts upon it. This courageous self-affirmation, which is surely a remedy for fear, is not selfishness, for self-affirmation includes both a proper self-love and a properly propositioned love of others. Erich Fromm has shown in convincing terms that the right kind of self-love and the right kind of love of others are independent.

Courage, the determination not to be overwhelmed by any object, however frightful, enables us to stand up to any fear. Many of our fears are not mere snakes under the carpet. Trouble is a reality in this strange medley of life, dangers lurk within the circumference of every action, accidents do occur, bad health is an ever-threatening possibility, and death is a stark, grim, and inevitable fact of human experience. Evil and pain in this conundrum of life are close to each of us, and we do both ourselves and our neighbors a great disservice when we attempt to prove that there is nothing in this world of which we should be frightened. These forces that threaten to negate life must be challenged by courage, which is the power of life to affirm itself in spite of life's ambiguities. This requires the exercise of a creative will that enables us to hew out a stone of hope from a mountain of despair.

Courage and cowardice are antithetical. Courage is an inner resolution to go forward in spite of obstacles and frightening situation; cowardice is a submissive surrender to circumstance. Courage breeds creative self-affirmation; cowardice produces destructive self-abnegation. Courage faces fear and thereby masters it. Courageous men never lose the zest for living even though their life situation is zestless; cowardly men, overwhelmed by the uncertainties of life, lose the will to live. We must constantly build dikes of courage to hold back the flood of fear.

III

Third, fear is mastered through love. The New Testament affirms, "There is no fear in love; but perfect love casteth out fear." The kind of love which led Christ to a cross and kept Paul unembittered amid the angry torrents of persecution is not soft, anemic, and sentimental. Such love confronts evil without flinching and shows in our popular parlance an infinite capacity "to take it." Such love overcomes the world even from a rough-hewn cross against the skyline.

But does love have a relationship to our modern fear of war, economic displacement, and racial injustice? Hate is rooted in fear, and the only cure for fear-hate is love. Our deteriorating international situation is shot through with the lethal darts of fear. Russia fears America, and America fears Russia. Likewise China and India, and the Israelis and the Arabs. These fears include another nation's aggression, scientific and technological supremacy, and economic power, and our own loss of status and power. Is not fear one of the major causes of war? We say that war is a consequence of hate, but close scrutiny reveals this sequence: first fear, then hate, then war, and finally deeper hatred. Were a nightmarish nuclear war to engulf our world, the cause would be not so much one nation hated another, but that both nations feared each other.

What method has the sophisticated ingenuity of modern man employed to deal with the fear of war? We have armed ourselves to the nth degree. The West and the East have engaged in a fever-pitched arms race. Expenditures for defense have risen to mountainous proportions, and weapons of destruction have been assigned priority over all other human endeavors. The nations have believed that greater armaments will cast out fear. But alas! They have produced greater fear. In these turbulent, panic-stricken days we are once more reminded of the judicious words of old, "Perfect love casteth out fear." Not arms, but love, understanding, and organized good-will can cast out fear. Only disarmament, based on good faith, will make mutual trust a living reality.

Our own problem of racial injustice must be solved by the same formula. Racial segregation is buttressed by such irrational fears of loss of preferred economic privilege, altered social status, intermarriage, and adjustment to new situations. Through sleepless nights and haggard days numerous white people attempt to combat these corroding fears by diverse methods. By following the path of escape, some seek to ignore the question of race relations and to close their mind to the issues involved. Others placing their faith in such legal maneuvers as interposition and nullification, counsel massive resistance. Still others hope to drown their fear by engaging in acts of violence and meanness toward their Negro brethren. But how futile are all these remedies! Instead of eliminating fear, they instill deeper and more pathological fears that leave the victims inflicted with strange psychoses and peculiar cases of paranoia. Neither repression, massive resistance, nor aggressive violence will casts out fear of integration; only love and goodwill can do that.

If our white brothers are to master fear, they must depend not only on their commitment to Christian love but also on the Christlike love which the Negro generates toward them. Only through our adherence to love and nonviolence will the fear in the white community be mitigated. A guilt-ridden white minority fears that if the Negro attains power, he will without restraint or pity act to revenge the accumulated injustices and brutality of the years. A parent, who has continually mistreated his son, suddenly realizes that he is now taller than the parent. Will the son use his new physical power to repay for all of the blows of the past?

Once a helpless child, the Negro has now grown politically, culturally, and economically. Many white men fear retaliation. The Negro must show them that they have nothing to fear, for the Negro forgives and is willing to forget the past. *The Negro must convince the white man that he seeks justice for both himself and the white man.* A mass movement exercising love and nonviolence and demonstrating power under discipline should convince the white community that were such a movement to attain strength its power would be used creatively and not vengefully.

What then is the cure of this morbid fear of integration? We know the cure. God help us to achieve it! Love casts our fear.

This truth is not without a bearing on our personal anxieties. We are afraid of the superiority of other people, of failure, and of the scorn or disapproval of those whose opinions we most value. Envy, jealousy, a lack of self-confidence, a feeling of insecurity, and a haunting sense if inferiority are all rooted in fear. We do not envy people and then fear them; first we fear them and subsequently we become jealous of them. Is there a cure for these annoying fears that pervert our personal lives? Yes, a deep and abiding commitment to the way of love. "Perfect love casteth out fear."

Hatred and bitterness can never cure the disease of fear; only love can do that. Hatred paralyzes life; love releases it. Hatred confuses life; love harmonizes it. Hatred darkens life; love illuminates it.

IV

Fourth, fear is mastered through faith. A common source of fear is an awareness of deficient resources and of a consequent inadequacy for life. All too many people attempt to face the tensions of life with inadequate spiritual resources. When vacationing in Mexico, Mrs. King and I wished to go deep-sea fishing. For reasons of economy, we rented an old and poorly equipped boat. We gave this little thought until, ten miles from shore, the clouds lowered and howling winds blew. Then we became paralyzed with fear, for we knew our boat was deficient. Multitudes of people are in a similar situation. Heavy winds and weak boats explain their fear.

Many of our abnormal fears can be dealt with by the skills of psychiatry, a relatively new discipline pioneered by Sigmund Freud, which investigates the subconscious drives of men and seeks to discover how and why fundamental energies are diverted into neurotic channels. Psychiatry helps us to look candidly at our inner selves and to search out the causes of our failures and fears. But much of our fearful living encompasses a realm where the service of psychiatry is ineffectual unless the psychiatrist is a man of religious faith. For our trouble is simply that we attempt to confront fear without faith; we sail through the stormy seas of life without adequate spiritual boats. One of the leading physicians in America has said, "The only known cure for fear is faith."

Abnormal fears and phobias that are expressed in neurotic anxiety may be cured by psychiatry; but the fear of death, nonbeing, and nothingness expressed in existential anxiety may be cured only by a positive religious faith.

A positive religious faith does not offer an illusion that we shall be exempt from pain and suffering, nor does it imbue us with the idea that life is a drama of unalloyed comfort and untroubled ease. Rather, it instills us with the inner equilibrium needed to face strains, burdens and fears that inevitably come, and assures us that the universe is trustworthy and that God is concerned.

Irreligion, on the other hand, would have us believe that we are orphans cast into the terrifying immensities of space in a universe that is without purpose or intelligence. Such a view drains courage and exhausts the energies of men. In his *Confession* Tolstoi wrote concerning the aloneness and emptiness he felt before his conversion:

> There was a period in my life when everything seemed to be crumbling, the very foundations of my convictions were beginning to give way, and I felt myself going to pieces. There was no sustaining influence in my life and there was no God there, so every night before I went to sleep, I made sure that there was no rope in my lest I be tempted during the night to hang myself from the rafters of my room; and I stopped from going out shooting lest I be tempted to put a quick end to my life and to my misery.

Like so many people, Tolstoi at that stage of his life lacked the sustaining influence which comes from the conviction that this universe is guided by a benign Intelligence whose infinite love embraces all mankind.

Religion endows us with the conviction that we are not alone in this vast, uncertain universe. Beneath an above the shifting sands of time, the uncertainties that darken our days, and the vicissitudes that cloud our nights is a wise and loving God. This universe is not a tragic expression of meaningless chaos but a marvelous display of orderly cosmos—"The Lord by wisdom hath founded the earth; by understanding hath he established the heavens." Man is not a wisp of smoke from a limitless smoldering, but a child created "a little lower than the angels." Above the manyness of time stands the one eternal God, with wisdom to guide us, strength to protect us, and love to keep us. His boundless love supports and contains us as a mighty ocean contains and supports the tiny drops of every wave. With a surging fullness he is forever moving toward us, seeking to fill the little creeks and bays of our lives with unlimited resources. This is religion's everlasting diapason, its eternal answer to the enigma of existence. Any man who fines this cosmic sustenance can walk the highways of life without the fatigue of pessimism and the weight of morbid fears.

Herein lies the answer to the neurotic fear of death that plagues so many of our lives. Let us face the fear that the atomic bomb has aroused with the faith that we can never travel beyond the arms of the Divine. Death is inevitable. It is a democracy for all of the people, not an aristocracy for some of the people—kings die and beggars die; young men die and old men die; learned men die and ignorant men die. We need not fear it. The God who brought our whirling planet from primal vapor and has led the human pilgrimage for lo these many centuries can most assuredly lead us through death's dark night into the bright daybreak of eternal life. His will is too perfect and his purposes are too extensive to be contained in the limited receptacle of time and the narrow walls of earth. Death is not the ultimate evil; the ultimate evil is to be outside God's love. We need not join the mad rush to purchase an earthly fallout shelter. God is our eternal fallout shelter.

Jesus knew that nothing could separate man from the love of God. Listen to his majestic words:.

> .. And fear not them which kill the body, but are not able to kill the soul; but rather fear him which is able to destroy both soul and body in hell. Are not two sparrows sold for a farthing? and one of them shall not fall on the ground without your Father. But the very hairs of your head are all numbered. Fear ye not therefore, ye are of more value than many sparrows.

Man, for Jesus, is not mere flotsam and jetsam in the river of life, but he is a child of God. Is it not unreasonable to assume that God, whose creative activity is expressed in an awareness of a sparrow's fall and the number of hairs on a man's head excludes from his encompassing love the life of man itself? The confidence that God is mindful of the individual is of tremendous value in dealing with the disease of fear, for it gives us a sense of worth, of belonging, and of at-homeness in the universe.

One of the most dedicated participants in the bus protest in Montgomery, Alabama, was an elderly Negro who we affectionately called Mother Pollard. Although poverty-stricken and uneducated, she was amazingly intelligent and possessed a deep understanding of the meaning of the movement. After having walked for several weeks, she was asked if she were tired. With ungrammatical profundity, she answered, "My feets is tired, but my soul is rested."

On a particular Monday evening, following a tension-packed week which included being arrested and receiving numerous threatening telephone calls, I spoke at a mass meeting. I attempted to convey an overt impression of strength and courage, although I was inwardly depressed and fear-stricken. At the end of the meeting, Mother Pollard came to the front of the church and said, "Come here, son." I immediately went to her and hugged her affectionately. "Something is wrong with you," she said. "You didn't talk strong tonight." Seeking further to disguise my fears, I retorted, "Oh, no, Mother Pollard, nothing is wrong. I am feeling fine as ever." But her insight was discerning. "Now you can't fool me," she said. "I knows something is wrong. Is it that we ain't doing things to please you? Or is it that the white folks is bothering you?" Before I could respond, she looked directly into my eyes and said, "I don told you we is with you all the way." Then her face became radiant and she said in words of quiet certainty, "But even if we ain't with you, God's gonna take care of you." As she spoke these consoling words, everything in me quivered and quickened with the pulsing tremor of raw energy.

Since that dreary night in 1956, Mother Pollard has passed on to glory and I have known very few quiet days. I have been tortured without and tormented within by the raging fires of tribulation. I have been forced to muster what strength and courage I have to withstand howling winds of pain and jostling storms of adversity. But as the years have unfolded the eloquently simple words of Mother Pollard have come back again and again to give light and peace and guidance to my troubled soul. "God's gonna take care of you."

This faith transforms the whirlwind of despair into a warm and reviving breeze of hope. The words of a motto which a generation ago were commonly found on the wall in the homes of devout persons need to be etched on our hearts:

> Fear knocked at the door.
> Faith answered.
> There was no one there.

Martin Luther King, Jr., "Antidotes for fear," is reprinted by arrangement with The Heirs to the Estate of Martin Luther King Jr., c/o Writers House as agent for the proprietor, New York, NY.

Copyright © 1963 by Dr. Martin Luther King, Jr. Renewed © 1991 by Coretta Scott King.

Appendix F

It's Time to End Any Level of Federal Marijuana Prohibition

Trevor Burrus

Published by the Cato Institute, December 2, 2020, and available at It's Time to End Any Level of Federal Marijuana Prohibition | Cato Institute

Either today or later this week, the House will likely take the historic step and actually hold a vote on whether to deschedule marijuana from the Controlled Substances Act (CSA). In addition, the Marijuana Opportunity Reinvestment and Expungement (MORE) Act would expunge low-level marijuana offenses and impose a 5 percent federal sales tax. The bill is unlikely to get past the Republican Senate, and there are many other proposals—some with the seeming support of President–elect Biden—that would *re*schedule rather than *de*schedule the plant. But descheduling—removing the drug from the CSA entirely—is the only sensible path forward for marijuana reform, not rescheduling—moving the drug to a different section of the CSA. Like alcohol, the federal government should have very little involvement in regulating marijuana.

The CSA separates drugs into five schedules based on the perceived danger. Schedule I has the supposed worst drugs, those that have no accepted medical uses and a high potential for abuse. That's where you'll find heroin, ecstasy, LSD, psilocybin, and, yes, marijuana.

Unlike drugs that are discrete, scientifically identifiable compounds, such as diacetylmorphine (heroin), MDMA (ecstasy), or LSD, marijuana is a whole plant containing a complex assortment of psychoactive and therapeutic compounds giving it a broad range of effects. Many of those substances are capable of being refined out of the plant and put into different uses, such as salves, candies, therapeutic oils, and of course smokable substances. To place the whole plant into any schedule of the CSA affects the use of every substance that is derived from the plant, whether it is psychoactive THC or therapeutic CBD or CBN.

The analogy to alcohol is apt. Schedule I drugs are those with no accepted medical uses and a high potential for abuse. Given that language, where should alcohol be scheduled if we were to try to fit it into the scheduling system? Seems like there's a good case for it being in Schedule I. Except for odd circumstances, doctors don't tend to prescribe shots of bourbon, and the high potential for abuse of alcohol is obvious.

But what is "alcohol," and what would it mean if "alcohol" were put under the CSA? That word encompasses everything from Uncle Clarence's moonshine to White Claw, from Bacardi 151 to a glass of champagne. Any reasonable regulation of alcohol would require acknowledging that a shot of 151 is not the same as a wine spritzer. Because of that wide variance, putting "alcohol" in the CSA would be absurd. The substance should be regulated on a state and local level to ensure that people can use the drug responsibly within reasonable limits for public safety.

States already regulate alcohol this way. Everclear 190, a potent spirit that is 95 percent pure alcohol, is illegal in 14 states. Other states regulate shot size, drink style, and of course what days and hours bars can be open. This type of more localized regulation makes sense for such a broadly used and diverse substance as alcohol.

And it makes sense for marijuana. Not only does marijuana have at least as much variance in product type and potency as alcohol, but it has many more therapeutic and medicinal uses. Some would say that means marijuana should be rescheduled to a lower level of the CSA that acknowledges medical uses. Schedule II, for example, contains morphine, fentanyl, methamphetamine, and cocaine, which, despite their dangers, have acknowledged medical uses.

But rescheduling marijuana would solve few of the issues that plague recreational and medicinal users in the states that have legalized, and it certainly wouldn't solve the challenges that face the growing cannabis industry. Unauthorized possession of cocaine, despite its acknowledged medical uses, still carries stiff penalties under federal law. Similarly, if a state wishes to recognize a broad set of medicinal marijuana uses, the federal government is in no way obligated to comport itself to that state's judgment. Finally, rescheduling, without more, won't solve the longstanding problems with banking faced by cannabis-based businesses.

Federal marijuana prohibition in America began as a largely unnoticed tax act in 1937. It seems clear that many members of Congress who voted for the law didn't even realize that marijuana and cannabis are the same thing. Over the next decades, federal and state marijuana prohibition have ruined countless lives, orders of magnitude more than the lives ruined by the actual drug. It's time to take the sensible step and get the federal government out of marijuana prohibition altogether.

This article is reprinted under a license from Creative Commons Corporation, available at Creative Commons — Attribution 4.0 International — CC BY 4.0.

About the Author

James E. Scheuermann received his B.A. (in history) and his Ph.D. (in philosophy) from the University of Chicago. He received his J.D. from the University of Pittsburgh School of Law. He is a former high school and college teacher and for more than thirty years has been a practicing lawyer with a major international law firm. He is the author of numerous articles in scholarly philosophy journals, law reviews, and other legal publications.

www.ingramcontent.com/pod-product-compliance
Lightning Source LLC
Chambersburg PA
CBHW030142240426
43672CB00005B/229